Memories

of

Bromley

The publishers would like to thank the following companies for their

support in the production of this book

Main Sponsor
Allied Bakeries

FW Berringer & Company

AG Bishop

JW Bollom & Co Limited

Bromley College of Further and Higher Education

Bromley Court Hotel

Coates Lorilleux

Churchill Insurance

Glaxo Wellcome

MS Instruments Plc

Maunsell Limited

Paramount Plastics

Pearce Bros Builders Limited

Voyce of Bromley

Wellers Solicitors

First published in Great Britain by True North Books Limited
England HX5 9AE
01422 377977

ISBN 1 903204 21 6
Text, design and origination by True North Books Limited
Printed and bound by The Amadeus Press Limited

Memories

of

Bromley

Edited by Muriel Mudie

Contents

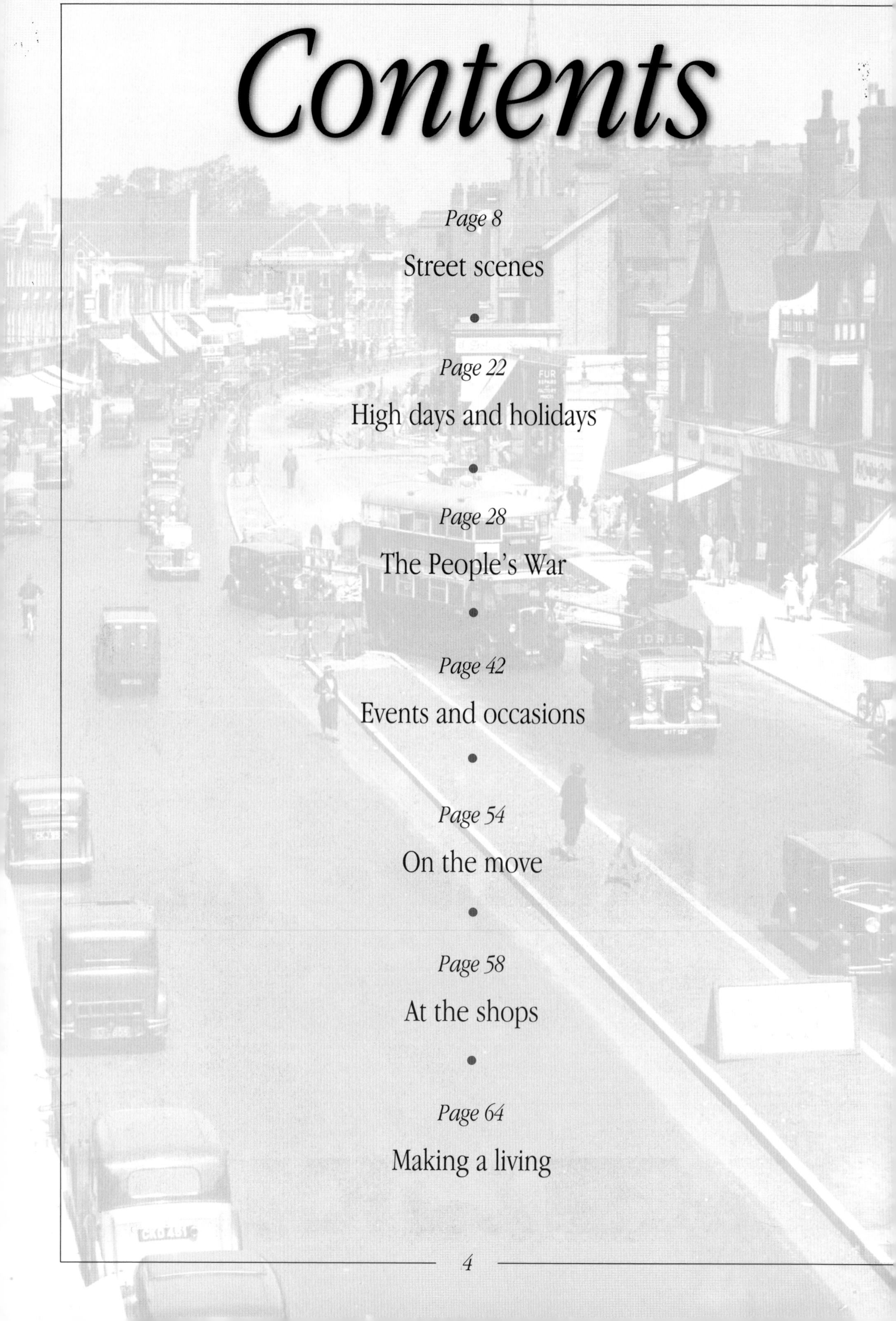

Page 8

Street scenes

•

Page 22

High days and holidays

•

Page 28

The People's War

•

Page 42

Events and occasions

•

Page 54

On the move

•

Page 58

At the shops

•

Page 64

Making a living

Bromley through the ages

Over the course of many centuries the fortunes of Bromley were closely inter-twined with those of the Bishops of Rochester. Ethelbert, King of Kent, made a grant of land in 862AD, land that was described as 'heath where the broom grows' - or 'broom leigh' - in other words Bromley. The Manor of Bromley came into the possession of the Bishops of Rochester in the eleventh century, remaining there until 1845. A Bishop's Palace was soon established, to be entirely rebuilt in 1775, and now forming the nucleus of the Civic Centre. Within the Palace grounds was a well which was reputed to have curative properties, dedicated to St Blaise. In a minor way, then, Bromley became a visiting place for pilgrims. Meanwhile the little rural settlement of Bromley began to develop around the present-day Market Square. In 1205 King John granted a charter to the Bishop of Rochester which allowed a weekly market on Tuesdays. A second charter from Henry VI, in 1447, changed market day to Thursday, and allowed fairs in February and July. The parish church of St Peter and St Paul was established in the thirteenth century on the site of a norman predecessor, with the tower being added in the fourteenth century.

Families gather for a Victory in Europe party at Clock House Road, Beckenham on May 30th 1945

Slow growth took place, although by 1662 it is reckoned that the population was still less than 700. Another substantial building, however, was soon to be added when in 1666, John Warner, Bishop of Rochester, left £8,500 in his will to build a college, or almshouse, for 'twenty poore widowes of Orthodox and Loyalle clergyman'. Bromley College was built between 1670 and 1672, and Bromley itself at this date consisted of little more than the High Street, from the College to just beyond the market place. The College, much extended, still remains and its original function has been largely preserved, housing mainly clergy widows plus retired clergymen.

The Coaching Age

If Bromley had a certain sleepy, ecclesiastical atmosphere about it, then matters began to liven up towards the end of the eighteenth century. Favourably situated on the London to Hastings turnpike road, Bromley became a busy and important coaching stop as road travel began to increase. There were three coaching inns, the White Hart became prominent. The Bell was another, becoming the Royal Bell when royal coaches began changing horses

there. Some of the coach travel was generated by the presence of James Scott's premises opposite the Bell. The service was called Scott's Coaches. This famous surgeon practised in Bromley from 1794 to 1829, his speciality being the saving of limbs that might otherwise have been amputated. Nevertheless Bromley remained a small country town. Even Lower High Street, descending towards the present-day Bromley South station, was bordered by the Bromley House and Bromley Lodge estates. For real growth, the railway age was to be the crucial factor.

The Railway Age - Take Off!

In 1858 the railway arrived at what is now called Bromley South station, Bromley North being opened in 1878. From being a small market town, Bromley rapidly developed as a Kentish suburb of London. The impact was immediate as new families arrived from London, Kent and further afield. The lure of living in an attractive and healthy country area, whilst being able to commute to London for work, proved irresistible. By 1900 housing and commercial premises were almost continuous up Lower High Street to Market Square. Population growth was

Bromley High Street in a picture dating from 1967

now astonishing - from 5,500 in 1861; to 15,000 in 1881; to 33,500 in 1911. Some of the land for development was made available by the purchase of Bromley Palace by the wealthy businessman, Coles Child, in 1845. Both he and his son, of the same name, sold off some of the large estate to builders. Similarly, Bickley Park was turned into building plots - the area becoming known as New Bromley. Growth, of course, brought problems pertaining to drainage, sewage disposal, water supply, street lighting and the provision of roads and schools. A Local Board was elected in 1867, to be replaced by an Urban District Council in 1894. Bromley received its charter as a borough in 1903. Amidst all the excitement and change of the nineteenth century, Bromley's most famous son was born at number 47 High Street in 1866 - HG Wells.

Conflict and Change

The twentieth century brought the Great War from 1914 to 1918, and a monument on Martin's Hill to over 850 fallen heroes from Bromley. World War II was to put civilians in the front line as the locality found itself beneath the route of German bombers heading for London. Also the close proximity of Biggin Hill airfield ensured the attention of enemy aircraft. In 1940 the people of Bromley and district watched their own destiny, and that of many others, decided in the skies above them in the epic Battle of Britain. For the rest of the war, the area was hit by bombs, flying bombs and V2 rockets, causing hundreds of deaths.

Since the end of the war, the rise of mass car ownership since the 1960s has transformed people's lives, just as the railways did a century earlier. But a new battle had to be fought - to prevent the heart of Bromley being strangled by traffic congestion and choked by fumes. The completion of a relief road in 1992, Kentish Way, allowed the central section of High Street to be fully pedestrianised later. The revolution in shopping habits is best expressed by the huge Glades Shopping Centre, opened in 1991. Meanwhile a quiet administrative revolution has resulted in that tiny Manor of Bromley, created so many centuries ago, extending its boundaries. The London Borough of Bromley has included Hayes and Keston since 1934. It was joined by Beckenham, Biggin Hill, Chislehurst, the Crays, Orpington and Penge in 1964.

Street scenes

A fascinating shot of Bromley High Street in 1900 evokes a time when horse-drawn traffic reigned supreme. Although Queen Victoria still had a year to live, the dress fashion on view is what one would term Edwardian. The Star and Garter Inn sign is very prominent to the right, but only a hint is given (the top of the dome) of the adventurous architecture of its exterior. That landmark sign and that eye-catching design, giving the impression of an 'olde worlde' hostelry, are still to be seen today, but the Star and Garter was only built in 1898. The mock Tudor design was the work of Berney and Sons for a Croydon firm of brewers, Nalder & Collyer. Similarly the nearby Royal Bell Hotel was also built in 1898, this time in Georgian style, but with some justification, for its predecessor on the site had been an eighteenth century coaching inn. A variety of shops existed in this part of High Street in 1900 including George Weeks & Son (ironmongers), William Hobbs (farrier) and the Archer Cycle Works. The name of Pamphilon has recently been restored to part of the premises which, in 1900, belonged to Pamphilon & Son, wine merchants and cigar importers. The camera angle on this photograph is looking northwards, and that end of High Street provides another link with 1900, for the Swan & Mitre public house retains its original early nineteenth century exterior.

Below: Beckenham Lane, Shortlands, seems to belong to another world in this shot from 1923 in view of the dress and the lack of traffic, and in many ways it did. Very few people owned a motor-car, and so children could play alongside the street in relative safety, as they are doing here. Similarly there was little danger from wagons, for the main mode of local commercial transport was the horse and cart, and one can be seen approaching in the distance. In general the whole scene has an air of tranquillity and calm, far removed from today's busy pace of life and huge volumes of traffic. The Shortlands Post Office sign can be seen, with its associated Telegraph Office, both key communications links for the people of the area. The great spur to the development of Shortlands had been the arrival of the West End and Crystal Palace Railway

in May 1858. A station to serve Bromley had opened at Shortlands, and local tradesmen saw the possibilities of providing for passing trade. In this way Shortlands village began to grow. Prior to this the area had been mainly pasture land, with a marshy area to the north of the river known as Frog Island.

Bottom: Hayes means 'village on the heath', and although only 12 miles from the centre of London, it was still being described as a place of rural delight in 1900. This description no doubt partly owed itself to the existence of Hayes Common, 220 acres of wild heathland just to the south of the village. The photograph shows Station Approach looking south, with the centre of Hayes having rather more of a town than a village appearance. The station was opened in 1882 and, unlike some areas, the arrival of the railway did not have dramatic immediate impact. Hayes was still only a small community of around 830 people in 1900, although it was a popular destination for London day trippers and the line was well used by commuters. In fact, in 1933 the only buildings in the area of the photograph were the station and the New Inn opposite. By 1936, however, Station Approach was flanked by shops in the wake of the electrification of the Southern Railway. Some clue to the date of the photograph lies in the fact that the shops are certainly there, but the appearance of the vehicles gives the picture an air of not much later than this.

The vehicles on High Street give a 1930s feel to this shot. One of the most interesting features is the Methodist Church on the right. This fine Gothic structure was opened in 1875, a culmination of a process which began with a small chapel at Widmore Green in 1776, moving through a larger Zion Chapel to the rear of 66 to 67 High Street in the 1820s, to the edifice which is pictured. The house, said to be the manse to the church, to the right of the church dated from much the same time, and on photographs from the 1880s it is fascinating to see

how rural the area still looked, with trees facing the Methodist Church across the High Street. Later shops, such as the Wallpaper Stores, were built in front of the houses, thus preserving them. This 1930s photograph, however, has intimations of the future as well as evidence of the past. 'Esso - World's Most Advanced Petrols', is proudly proclaimed from the gable end in the background, a reminder that the age of the motor car was gathering momentum. Also the van to the left belonged to the Henfreys, electrical wiring contractors. Electricity - the growing energy and light source of the future.

Right: In 1935 the local council at Bromley approved a major redevelopment scheme at a cost of £36,250, to be supplemented by Ministry of Transport funding. The focus of the work was to be the widening of High Street, along with improvements over the railway bridge at Bromley South Station and along Masons Hill to Westmoreland Road. This photograph shows the work well underway, and the number of vehicles visible suggests that growing pressure of motor traffic was at least one of the motivating factors. Another 'spin off' was to be new shops and showrooms as advertised by Baxter, Payne and Lepper, estate agents. Some interesting features of the time include the overhead lighting system, the delivery bike propped against a lamp standard and a fascinating view of the steps of a rear entry bus. Bromley South Station can be seen at far left, and if cars were making an impact in the 1930s, the same could be said of the arrival of the railway at Bromley in 1858. For example the substantial building beyond the station, the Railway Signal public house, was opened to cater for the railway trade. It was closed in 1987, the site later becoming part of a car-park.

Below: The Beckenham High Street traders' names on view might give some readers a clue to the date of this picture, although around 1950 has been suggested. It was a time when WC Wykes was appealing to a sense of tradition and continuity in proudly declaring to have been, 'Hosier, Hatter and Tailor For Men & Their Sons'. Close by was the Cosy Cafe, whilst opposite was the shop of TR Baker. In the background, on the bend, stands the substantial building housing the Three Tuns public house, which was to be re-invented much later as the Rat and Parrot. Speaking of names, Beckenham has ancient origins and its name, like the settlement itself, has evolved slowly since 862 AD, when it was mentioned in a charter of King Ethelbert as 'Beohhahem' - try saying that after visiting the Rat and Parrot! Amidst slow change, of course, there are always spurts of rapid development, and the arrival of the railway line from London in 1857 had a great impact. Between 1841 and 1881, the population of Beckenham increased from 1,600 to 13,000, reflecting a large amount of building. The High Street has remained at the heart of Beckenham's commercial life through all the centuries of change.

Above: A fairly quiet scene in 1935 is shown here as High Street, Bromley, is dominated by pedestrians and a butcher's delivery boy. There was no mistaking schoolboys either in those days, for the two in the photograph are donned in regulation uniform from top to toe. And woe betide any schoolboy who was caught with as much as his cap askew by a teacher! Although quiet for the moment, changes were afoot for this area, for in 1935 a £36,250 improvement scheme had been approved. It included the railway bridge featured here. Bromley South Station was just off camera to the left. It would be difficult to overestimate the influence of the arrival of the railway in 1858 on the town's life. The swift link with London allowed people to work there and live in the pleasant retreat of Bromley. The rapid growth in the town's population now began. The Railway Signal public house - the rounded building to the left - was opened to service commuters. Edwin A Cornwall, coal merchant, could work straight out of the railway yards. These junctions from this viewpoint have changed out of all recognition since 1935, the most eye-catching feature now being Churchill Court, the headquarters of Churchill Insurance.

Top: So much of this fascinating old picture of Bromley's High Street in 1935 tells a story of the time. The advertisement for Morley's Pianos is very appropriately attached to the College of Music. Howard Morley Phillips and Co had a very reputable music store and showrooms on High Street, and were always anxious to point out that their piano tuners were experienced in 'London Houses'. They were also sole agents for the Imperial Orchestra Band and many other local bands, able to perform at a range of functions in 'Hungarian Military Uniform or Evening Dress as desired'. Entertainment of another kind was also booming in the 1930s - the cinema. The Gaumont Palace at Lewisham, showing 'Cardinal Richelieu', declares prominently above the billboard that it is a Super Cinema, with seating for 3,000, along with a cafe-restaurant and lounges and notable for its own ballroom, a Victor Silvester dancing school. These were days of soaring ambitions for cinema entrepreneurs! Of course there was no need to go to Lewisham, for the same programme was showing at the Grand, Bromley. An alternative was to visit the Palais in High Street and see the famous James Cagney in 'G - Men'. With a capacity of 731, this was a much cosier place, and in later years it was to be reincarnated as first the Pullman, and later the Astor.

Left: The section of Croydon Road between its junction with Upper Elmers End Road and Eden Park Avenue is featured in a photograph from around the 1950s. An array of trading names that were once very familiar, and one or two that still are, greets the eye - Coupland, United Dairies, Findlay, Shepherds, Dewhurst, Wymans, Kennedy etc. If the view is very much an urban one, however, Elmers End was still being described as a village in the 1950s, a place with its own distinctive, separate identity. That was very much the case about a century earlier when Elmers End comprised two farms, Elmer Lodge, the William IV public house and a few shops and cottages. As for nearby Eden Park, this was once part of the great Kelsey estate of the Burrell family, the name deriving from William Eden, Lord Auckland, who died in 1814. The name of Elmers End has not been a constant one in the district's history, for at various times it has been known as Elms End and Aylmers End. Any peaceful tranquillity that might have been found at Elmers End was rudely destroyed when German bombs began to fall from the summer of 1940. On September 15th 1940, the local station was paralysed by an unexploded bomb and on July 18th 1944, there were 17 deaths when a flying bomb hit Elmers End bus garage.

Above: The flags are flying bravely on both the Harrison Gibson and Wolfe & Hollander Home Furnishing stores as the camera takes a long view southwards along High Street in 1935. Advertising of a more modest kind is visible on G Boyce's handcart in the foreground, on the rear of which is featured the name Hovis. Modest or not, Hovis is still with us, whereas all the other pictured High Street names have now gone - the Fifty Shilling Tailor, Eve Sheldon, the Twelve & Nine Shoe Store and the two furniture retailers. Harrison Gibson suffered a disastrous fire in 1968, but was on the brink of being taken over by the Army and Navy Stores. The Wolfe & Hollander building was brand new at the time of this photograph, 1935, and was to be modernised and enlarged by about a third in 1955, the extra space being utilised for hardware. The Wolfe & Hollander name disappeared in 1971, however, when the business was taken over by John Peters Furnishing Stores. Further down High Street, it is possible to see again the publicity for Morley's Pianos, close to the College of Music. The Morley Phillips & Co, still exist in lewisham, later known as robert morley, music stores were familiar High Street landmarks in this era.

Above: Change is a constant factor in town centres, and yet some periods of time are distinguished by specially radical alterations in a townscape. The date of this view northwards along High Street is 1967, and the area was on the brink of one such upheaval. It was not just that 7,000 square feet of new shop and office space was being offered by Selway Bamber to the far right of the picture. Attention was being focused too on the fine building to the left of High Street, with the balustrade and finely carved frontage. This, the Central Library, had stood on this spot since 1906, but would soon have to make way for the ambitious development scheme of the Churchill Library-Theatre. The books would be cleared out in 1968 and demolition would take place in 1969. The towering new structure, however, would not be completed until 1977. There are always survivors, however, amidst change. The building with the tall gable and chimney to the left of the old Library, 'Ravensfell', still stands today. It was built as a large detached villa for an Australian merchant in 1858.

Above right: The distinctive double bend of Beckenham High Street is seen from the vantage point of the tower of St Edmund's Roman Catholic Church around 1938, the year of its completion on this site. The High Street saw much development in the 1930s, and many of the buildings would have been relatively new at this date. Beer and stout seem to dominate the advertisement hoardings, which is appropriate enough considering that a dray wagon is delivering at the nearby Three Tuns public house. Between the hoardings and the large structure of the pub is Austin's shop, a building of great interest. It was built in the seventeenth century as a gardener's cottage and had become a butcher's shop by 1850. This it remained until, sadly, Austin's had to be demolished in 1959 because of woodworm damage. As High Street bends to the left, the white gable end of an equally interesting building is visible, the George Inn, Beckenham's oldest public house. It is known that in 1662 the landlord of the time paid the 'hearth tax'. The landlord of around 1715 was quite an entrepreneur, running a stagecoach twice weekly to London. Exciting events took place in 1835 when church-wardens raided the inn to catch out miscreants drinking during church services!

Right: Market Square, Bromley, in October 1960 presents a view which is at once familiar and yet nostalgic. The name of David Greig, in when gregs moved out, boldly displayed on the wrought iron railings above the Morris Minor, and a household name for meat and groceries, no longer features in the commercial life of the town. There was reputedly a marriage between a Greig and a Sainsbury - and indeed there never seemed to be both in the same town. Bromley had Greig for many years with Sainsbury's only moving in when Greig's moved out. Facing the camera, the name of F Medhurst was equally prominent in Bromley at this time. Founded in 1879 at 44 High Street, the shop had been extended by 1900 to embrace the property up to number 51, and Bromley's first department store had been born. The whole building was pulled down in 1927 and rebuilt as what is now Allders. Fred Medhurst's was still an integral part of the Bromley shopping scene for almost 20 years to come after this photograph was taken. Celebrating its centenary in 1979, the store stressed a new range of furnishings, fittings and clothing as would befit a 1980s Superstore. The name of Allders replaced that of F Medhurst in 1980, although the old name can still be seen, carved high up on the stonework of the building. The final name from the past is the reference to the White Hart on the street nameplate at bottom left. This famous old inn, dating back at least to 1509, was to be demolished in 1964.

Below: Masons Hill, as it swings right into the High Street, is joined first by Westmoreland Road at the bottom left, and then by Simpsons Road higher up. A good deal has changed at this junction since 1960, the date of this shot. Bromley was on the verge of the 'swinging sixties', but this scene is now one which seems to belong very much to a different age, especially the little hut on the left in which HV Dawes carried out his footwear repairs. Just above this hut are advertisements for two disinguished names in the bicycle world - Raleigh and Rudge - but the shape of things to come in town centres is best expressed by the two approaching vehicles. The Morris and Austin vans herald the huge rise in car ownership in the 1960s, with all the associated problems of congested urban centres. However, the photograph contains echoes of a pre-1960 world as well. The very name Masons Hill is derived from the fact that the area was once noted for its gravel pits which provided materials for road making, although brickmaking was the main industry. As for Simpsons Road, it took its name from a nearby fortified and moated house, Simpson's Place, which was no more than a haunted ruin by the early 1800s.

The traffic is fairly light on Orpington High Street, and the vehicles on view suggest a date somewhere in the 1950s for this photograph. The shop names of Lowaters and AT Trevillion catch the eye to the left, whilst the well-known name of David Greig is prominent on the wagon to the right. It is difficult to imagine that only 50 years earlier Orpington was a self-contained little village, but one that had already been affected by the arrival of the railway. In the 1880s there were 13 trains to London stopping at Orpington on weekdays, and commuting became a new part of everyday life for some. It can be no accident that the population increased by one third between 1881 and

1891, from 3,050 to 4,100. This was nothing, of course, as against the growth of Orpington in the twentieth century. If shopping along Orpington High Street in the 1950s appears to have been a fairly peaceful and relaxing affair, people were no doubt glad of it. Only a few years earlier bombs had been falling in the area. For example, in September 1940, land mines fell in Broadcroft Road, and in St Mary Cray and Petts Wood, killing several people. In the last stages of the war, a V2 rocket killed seven people at Court Road, Orpington, in January 1945. Another V2, the last one of the war, killed a resident of Court Road in March 1945 - the last victim in Britain of enemy air attack.

Bottom: The tail-end of a Morris Minor flits past the War Memorial as it negotiates the roundabout at the end of Orpington High Street. The date appears to be sometime in the 1950s, or early 60s, a time when the years of post-war austerity were beginning to be left behind. Not that the memories of war can be left behind just as easily, and the cenotaph was a constant reminder of the human losses of World War I. It was with the need in mind for another memorial, in commemoration of those from Orpington who had lost their lives in the second great conflict, that a public meeting had been convened in 1945. Out of this a decision had been made to open up the Priory Gardens as a place of remembrance. This remained the position for many years, but in the late 1990s Orpington`s Royal British Legion began a campaign for a memorial that would fully honour the 431 local war-dead from World War II and later conflicts. An appeal was launched for the money that would be needed to pay for engraved granite plinths to be added to the existing cenotaph - a sum of over £20,000. Fortunately the Catford firm of Francis Chappell & Son made a tremendous contribution by freely donating the stone and the engraving of names on the eight plaques. In August 1999 the solemn ceremony of unveiling the plaques took place after a parade of 400 people, led by the veterans of the British Legion.

Right: Simpsons Road and Masons Hill converge in a photograph taken in 1960. The Times Building can be seen in the background, whilst the business names of around that time include Chas Seeley, whose very eye-catching sign shows that he was in the dentures line, and Carter, Law & Leech, Estate Agents. Further to the left along Simpsons road, however, Bert's Dining Rooms have clearly seen better days. One of the two ladies passing these rather battered premises carries the type of little wicker shopping basket which was so much in vogue in those days. Another mark of the times is the little hut where HV Dawes carried out his footwear repairs. A cobbler, or some other tradesman, operating a one-man business in a tiny shop was certainly more common then than it is today. The posters on the wooden fence alongside the hut are in themselves 'period pieces'. Perhaps some readers may remember seeing 'Tiger Bay' at the Gaumont or Mario Lanza in the 'Seven Hills of Rome' at the Pullman. The latter had once been the Palais de Luxe Cinema, becoming the Pullman in 1954 and then the Astor in 1963.

The Market Square as seen in October 1960 reveals a trading name that was solid and established at this date, but was not to survive much longer. The photograph is dominated by the name of David Greig, a giant of the grocery trade for a good part of the twentieth century. Mrs DM Greig founded the company with a shop in Hornsey in 1870: the evidence still remains of when a branch was established in Market Square, Bromley, for the inscription 'David Greig 1912' is still to be seen high up on the white stone facade of the old premises. There were other Greigs in the borough, one at Masons Hill, one at Shortlands. In 1965, five years after this photograph was taken, the business underwent a major overhaul which involved the combination of the two shops into one large store. Although selling a range of groceries, meat was at the heart of the business, and in fact the company's slogan was, 'You cannot beat David Greig for bacon'. The store was also proud of the many products sold under the company's own Thistle Brand mark of quality, including Thistle Pies, Scotch Cake and Scotch House Tea. In spite of all the optimism, the premises were up for sale only eight years later, in 1973.

Spring was perhaps just about showing itself in Bromley on April 17th 1961, at least enough for people to think about outdoor activities. As a result a good crowd of onlookers has gathered around the pool at the Library Gardens to watch the little sailing boats. The pool had been created in 1933 after the purchase of Church House and its estate by the council in 1926, and sailing boats had been a popular pastime for youngsters ever since. A few people can be seen sitting on the grass, so maybe one or two picnics were on the cards as well. Unfortunately, however, by the 1960s the boating pond and the surrounding area was not always the scene of such pleasant, innocent pastimes.

Vandalism in the Library Gardens had become a matter of serious concern in the local council chambers, and in September 1963 the unique thatched bandstand was destroyed by fire for the second time in three years - the work of hooligans. Other recent acts of rowdyism had included seats being thrown in the lake, and damage to trees and shelters, but the estimated cost of replacing the bandstand was £2,000. On a more positive note, after the opening of the Churchill Library and Theatre complex in 1977, a major improvement scheme took place in the lower part of Church House Gardens - the 'dell' - in 1979. Linked with this was a redesign of the Library Gardens to cater for theatregoers, who are now also able to enjoy outdoor summer festivals.

High days & holidays

Above: There's plenty of high-jinks and 'horseplay' going on amongst these youngsters at Southlands Road Lido, Bromley, in 1963. As well as that, of course, there is just the pure enjoyment of swimming in the open air. Back in Victorian times, many local councils built swimming baths as part of a municipal drive to benefit public health and safety. There were many cases of people, particularly youngsters, either drowning or catching infectious diseases from swimming in the highly polluted rivers and canals of the day. It has to be said that this impulse was a slow moving one as far as Bromley was concerned, for it took 30 years to build a municipal swimming pool. It was opened in 1925 at a cost of £8,680, and was 150 feet in length and 60 feet in width (roughly 50 metres by 20 metres). Over 1,000 people turned up to see the opening ceremony, which was performed by the Mayor, Councillor E Ford Duncanson, and a gala followed. The Southlands Road Lido had a lifetime of 55 years before Bromley Council felt compelled to close the pool as part of a cash saving move in 1980.

This page: An air of calm and tranquillity pervades both these photographs as white sails gently scud across the surface of the boating pool. These shots were taken no later than about 1950, and there are no signs of any remote controlled, high-speed boats, with their accompanying noise. Instead sailboats slip noiselessly along in the beautiful setting of Church House Gardens, Bromley. Church House itself was destroyed by enemy bombing in April 1941 and its fine gardens were amalgamated with the Library Gardens. Church House was a fine building constructed in 1832 on the site of an older property off Church Road. Abel Moysey took a lease from the Bishop of Rochester's agent and was responsible for the lawns, shrubberies, fishponds and landscaping which forms such a beautiful feature of both photographs. One notable later occupant, between 1849 and 1863, was Mrs Scott, daughter-in-law of eminent Bromley surgeon, Mr James Scott. More beautiful grounds were laid out as a public park in 1906 when the Central Library was opened on the site of Neelgherries, which Mrs Emily Dowling had left to the people of Bromley in her will. It was in May 1926 that Church House and its grounds were purchased by the Bromley Council, who paid £7000 for an estate of over 11 acres, containing the house itself and three cottages. These were difficult times economically, but the council felt that it could not throw away such a golden opportunity to add to the amenities of the borough. Politically too these were turbulent times, the nine day General Strike having just ended, and Church House had been used as the headquarters for the maintenance of emergency services. The opening of the Church House grounds to the public in 1926 was a grand affair, with the Mayor, Councillor BA Glanville, doing the honours. Entertainment was provided by the Bromley and Bickley Band in the afternoon, and by the Bromley Silver Band in the evening. The Mayor declared that the grounds 'offer untold possibilities to the genius of our pleasure grounds superintendant'. In fact, what was entitled the Model Yachting Pond was to be one of the innovations, created in 1933 by the Bromley Unemployment Works Scheme. How many people of those who gathered together on that sunny afternoon in May 1926 could possibly have imagined the fate of Church House - to be bombed to ruins only 15 years later? Nevertheless, the grounds and 'Yachting Pond' lived on, to become part of the Library Gardens.

This page: A good cross-section of age, and both sexes, are represented in the quiet and beautiful setting of South Hill Wood Bowling Green, Bromley *(above)*. Probably the youngsters would stand it only for so long, however, unless they were allowed to retrieve one or two bowls from the gutter. Fascinating though the game may be to play, it is not exactly an absorbing spectator sport for the very young. The photograph dates from the late 1950s, for the South Hill Wood Bowling Club was founded in 1958. It set out with 65 members under the captain, Mr EW Newcombe, and the first game to be played on the green was watched by the Mayor and other civic personalities. The reason for the presence of these distinguished spectators was that the opening of the bowling green coincided with the official opening of South Hill Wood Park. As from May 2nd 1959, the residents

of the Shortlands and Park Langley area were able to enjoy their own park - the 15th in the borough of Beckenham. Councillor Miss KA Moore, the Mayor of Beckenham, did the honours when she formally unlocked the entrance gates on Westmoreland Road. The Mayor is partly obscured on the photograph

(below centre), although her regalia can be seen, as the small girl proudly presents a bouquet to one of the official party. This moment must have been rehearsed many times, and no doubt it is the effort of concentration that is making the little girl stick her tongue out! The land for the park had once formed the estate belonging to a large house, South Hill Wood. The purchase of the land and the creation of the park had cost Beckenham Council £29,000, the park comprising 10 acres of land, mostly heavily wooded. Besides a bowling green, the park opened with three hard tennis courts and it was planned that more should follow. The large house had been demolished apart from a section of it which was converted into a pavilion, where refreshments were served to the official opening party. The Westmoreland Road entrance gates had been designed to commemorate the Coronation of Queen Elizabeth II in 1953, and had been purchased by the £381 left over in the council's 'Coronation Fund'. Although small in comparison with some parks, South Hill Wood Park provided a pleasant little oasis in a natural landscape for the citizens of the area.

'At last...' was the headline in the local press which greeted the opening of the new Central Library in April 1977. No doubt the newness of the complex still caused passers-by in this rush hour scene of 1978 to glance upwards, for the tower block certainly dominates this part of the High Street, just as arguments and accusations had dominated this expensive and ambitious project. The fact that a three year scheme had extended to almost a decade explains the newspaper headline in question. Nevertheless the prevailing atmosphere was one of achievement when Bromley's Mayor, Alderman Mrs Stead, unveiled the plaque to mark the opening of the new Library. Borough Librarian, Mr Derek Laverick, claimed that the people of Bromley now had access to facilities which matched anything in the South of England, with 157,000 books, 14,000 items in the music section and a rich store of archival material. The Churchill Theatre was officially opened by Prince Charles on July 19th 1977. However, the first performance had taken place on July 4th. 'Mr Polly', based on the book by HG Wells, was chosen as a tribute to one of Bromley's famous sons. Unfortunately the Churchill Theatre had taken so long to complete that some who had booked tickets six years before had now died!

Above, both pictures: The creation of the Churchill Library-Theatre complex was one of the most ambitious projects ever undertaken by the Bromley Council, and these two photographs show the scheme at different stages of its evolution. The first view *(above)* is from the High Street in August 1972, and beneath a swathing of scaffolding the distinctive curve of the building is beginning to take definite shape. It is often difficult to measure the day-by-day progress of a new building, but a lapse of several months can tell a different story. The second view *(top)*, this time taken from the pleasant ornamental gardens, at a reverse angle, was captured in March 1973. The curve is now dominated by the skyward growth of the mighty tower block. The site of the new library had formerly accommo- dated the rather elegant building of the old Central Library, opened in 1906 with the aid of a gift of £7,500 from the philanthropist, Andrew Carnegie. A new library had been planned by the old Bromley Council before the creation of the London Borough of Bromley in 1965, and the new council decided to press on with the scheme. The demolition of the old Central Library began in 1969, and the book stock was housed in temporary accommodation on Tweedy Road. There is no doubt that Andrew Carnegie would have approved of bigger and better library facilities for the public of Bromley, but what he would have made of the controversy and bitterness that ran as a constant thread through the project is anyone's guess. In the first place, the scheme took much longer to complete than expected. Underground springs were encountered. The water table was only nine feet below the surface, and as the extent of underground accommodation required excavations of nearly 70 feet, this caused severe problems. Whereas three years had been envisaged for the entire scheme, it took four years to simply get up to High Street level. Naturally costs began to escalate, fuelled by the inflation of the 1970s, and accusations began to fly that the council was concealing the true costs and that the scheme was a 'white elephant' imposing a huge financial burden on the ratepayers. An original estimated cost of £1,725,000 for the whole complex in 1968 had swollen to over £4 million by 1977, although much of this was met by grants and the sale of shop leases. In spite of the controversy, the opening of both the Library and the Theatre in 1977 were occasions of great optimism and pride.

The People's War

The war on the Home Front took many forms between 1939 and 1945, and one of them was the drive to increase food production. The nation could no longer rely on imported food with German U-boats preying on merchant ships which, in any case, tended to be filled with essential war supplies. Many men were away fighting and so, as in the case of munitions production, women had to step in to fill the manpower gap. Hence the Women's Land Army was created, and a party of Land Girls can be seen here working at Hook Farm, on Bromley Common. Ernest Bevin, as Minister of Labour, had the job of deploying the million and a half women that were needed on the Home Front. The 80,000 women in the Land Army were sent wherever they were needed. The agricultural work was often hard and unfamiliar, but the sense of purpose and independence that Land Girls gained usually made up for this, along with the lifetime friendships that were forged. 'Dig for Victory', one of the most famous slogans of the war, was put to into operation as parks and flower beds were dug up and planted with vegetables. By April 1940 Bromley had 67 acres of allotments as compared to 37 acres before the war. Shortages persisted, however, and unless people had access to the 'black market', they had to cope with rations such as four ounces (112 grammes) of bacon, two ounces (56 grammes) of tea and half an egg per week!

Memories of *BROMLEY*

This page: The wreckage of what was once a house in Nightingale Lane, Bickley, forms the sad theme of this photograph, *(bottom)* an all-too common sight in the Bromley area during the second world war. Workmen are doing their best to salvage some of the contents. All this may well have been the work of a land mine which fell around midnight on September 18th 1940, killing nine people in the area of Nightingale Lane and Glenview Road. The second photograph *(below)* shows number 9 Dykes Way, Shortlands, in October 1940, and this gives the appearance of a house that has been evacuated after earlier bomb damage. With its close proximity to both London and Biggin Hill airfield, Bromley and district was bound to be in the thick of the action. Keston appears to have been the recipient of the first bomb in the locality, on July 30th 1940. Heavy

German attacks on Biggin Hill in August and September resulted in much damage as aircraft, parts of aircraft and jettisoned bombs came crashing down. However, Bromley itself was the target on September 6th 1940, when incendiary bombs ignited 48 fires in the town. The London blitz began on the next day and peaked on September 15th, when the air seemed to be full of fighting aircraft. At least 23 people were killed in Beckenham and Penge, including a number of patients at Parkfields Nursing Home in Crystal Palace Park Road. Those who lived through all this know now that they were witnesses to history in the making, but at the time fear and uncertainty must have been part of daily life. There were those who felt that public air-raid shelters, or Anderson shelters dug into gardens, did not offer enough protection, and they broke into Chislehurst Caves. By October 1940 over 8,000 people were sheltering there, who had been brought down by special train from London. Bromley's biggest air-raid of the war began on the night of April 16th 1941. Bromley received 198 bombs and by 10.30pm the town centre was ablaze. Amongst the buildings destroyed were eight churches including the Parish Church and Dunn's furniture store in Market Square. Later in the war there were some terrible individual incidents resulting from V1 flying bombs and V2 rockets. In August 1944 a V1 killed 44 people in a crowded restaurant in Beckenham (the Clock House pub was built on the site). In November 1944 a V2 killed 21 people in the Crooked Billet pub, Bromley. Within Beckenham, Bromley, Orpington, Penge and Chislehurst, the war accounted for 1,013 deaths and 6,331 injuries.

29

The proximity of Bromley to both Biggin Hill airfield and London meant that the area found itself in the front line of both the Battle of Britain and the blitz during World War II. And nobody could have been more in the front line than the inhabitants of number 26 Johnson Road when, on November 9th 1940, a German Heinkel III bomber crashed straight into the house. The very welcome success of the Spitfires and Hurricanes in the skies above South East England brought its own problems. On September 27th ten German planes had been brought down over Orpington and Chislehurst, and two more close to Biggin Hill. Nevertheless it must have come as a terrible shock to the residents of Johnson Road when the enemy aircraft crashed down on top of them, killing one person at number 26 and trapping two others in the ruins. An added danger was the fact that there were 29 unexploded bombs in the wreckage of the Heinkel, and the photograph shows some of these being examined by service personnel whilst a rescue squad surveys some of the damage nearby. The pilot and one crew member of the bomber were killed upon impact. Two more had bailed out, one of whom was killed, whilst the other was captured in Sundridge Park.

A good deal of preparation had gone into this Victory in Europe party at Clock House Road, Beckenham, on May 30th 1945. The tablecloth appears to be spotless (for how much longer?), the cakes and sandwiches are piled high, cut flowers have been neatly arranged and huge flags have been procured from somewhere. Amongst the workers standing at the rear was Mrs Winifred Campbell, ninth from the left. Perhaps someone may recognise himself or herself from the photograph, or remember one of the many street parties that took place for weeks after VE Day, May 8th 1945. Amongst the parties that took place, Henry Street was considered to be one of the best decorated in Bromley. The children of Godwin Road received either a victory beaker or a leather purse. Belgian evacuee children joined in the fun and entertainment at Park End. A bonfire in Palace View, Bromley, attracted a large crowd who cheered as an effigy of Hitler was thrown onto the flames. The more solemn aspect of Victory in Europe was reflected by the thousands who attended an open-air service at Queens Mead on May 9th. Thanksgiving was mingled with sadness, for the war had taken its toll in many ways on the people of Bromley and the surrounding area.

This page: A welcome day of sunshine has made it all worthwhile for the people of Recreation Road, Shortlands, in this happy scene captured in August 1945 *(below)*. This was a true street party, for which the weather is so important, and the children are posing long enough for a photograph before tucking into the 'goodies'. The same party atmosphere prevails in the second photograph *(bottom)*, and the same weather, but this time the scene is Dykes Way, Shortlands. It looks as if the vicar is among those who have bagged a place at 'top table', in the centre of the picture, whilst the gentleman at the rear looks as if he is guardian of the drinks supplies. It is a fair bet that much of the hard work in preparing the feast had fallen to the ladies in the 'pinnies' standing behind the tables, and that the washing up would be their

lot too. The occasion for both those street parties was the surrender of Japan and a total end to the second world war. There will still be plenty of people in Bromley and district who remember those momentous days, and some who might even spot younger versions of themselves on either of these photographs. VJ (Victory over Japan) Day fell officially on August 15th 1945, but was not greeted by the same scenes of wild enthusiasm as VE (Victory in Europe) Day had been in May. With the excitement and fear of the struggle with Germany over, people had begun to realise that there was a hard road ahead. Rationing, for example, did not fully end until 1954. There was also the realisation of the huge loss and suffering that the war had caused across the world. At a personal level, grief at the loss of loved ones did not end with the close of the war.

Nevertheless, street parties abounded throughout the Bromley area during the last two weeks of August, principally for the children. Those of Pope Road, Bromley Common, were entertained by a conjuror, whilst those of Pickhurst Mead, Hayes, had a Punch and Judy show, a treasure hunt and fairy lights after dusk. The Mayor and Mayoress, Councillor and Mrs A Collins, described the Victory Party put on by the children of Wharton Road and neighbouring streets as one of the best they had seen. With rationing still in force, providing party food to hungry children was only achieved, in the words of one organiser, 'by the pooling of food resources'.

Bread - the staff of life

Bread - the staff of life. Where would we be without bread to make sandwiches, mop up our gravy or to make our breakfast toast? Bread has been known for thousands of years, baked by housewives (or perhaps that should be cave-wives) since time immemorial. So important is the idea of bread and home that even the very word 'man' itself is ultimately derived from one of our ancient words for loaf.

Primitive ways of making bread can still be seen today in less developed parts of the world with unleavened dough baked on flat heated stones. Who first learned to add yeast to dough in order to allow fermentation to take place and let the dough 'rise' before baking is beyond recorded history - but the process was already well established in Mesopotamia and the Mediterranean in classical times.

For housewives making bread has always been a hard if worthwhile task. How many husbands coming home from the fields and forests, ravenous with hunger, salivated as they sniffed the air detecting the welcoming scent of newly baked bread waiting for them on their return?

No doubt thanks and appreciation were profuse but that still did not take the hard work out of the process. What housewives wanted was someone else to do the job for them. That demand, and the emergence of cities in the Near East, led eventually to specialisation and the arrival of the professional baker. Fresh bread daily was the watchword of those early bakers just as it is today. Bakers worked throughout the night baking bread so that it would be ready for sale first thing each morning.

And for those who still preferred their own recipes but could not be bothered to make a fire in order to do the baking themselves, bakers offered another service - bring your own dough and we'll bake your bread for you! Such a service persisted down the centuries and was still common in England until relatively recent times: in some cases a wise precaution since the adulteration of flour by any number of cheap substitutes such as chalk, straw and dust by some unscrupulous bakers persisted far into the 19th century.

In Britain small corner shop bakers remained the dominating force in bread making until at least the second world war, but major changes in production capacity meant they would be progressively challenged by large commercial bakeries operating on an industrial scale.

Above: An advertisement for Weston's confectionery.
Below: The confectionery department in the 1940s.

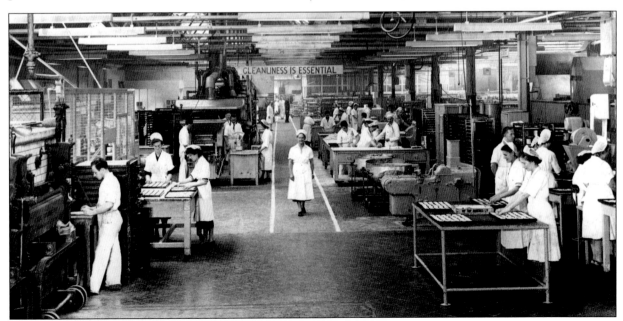

Allied bakeries was part of the Weston family baking empire. William Weston had been born in London in humble circumstances before emigrating to Canada in the 19th century. In Toronto his son George would transform the family fortunes. At the age of ten George started work as a baker's delivery boy: at the age of 17 he opened his own bakery. George then realised that the big money was to be made selling bread from door to door. By the time he sold his business in 1911 George Weston had become a millionaire. George then made another fortune after starting a biscuit factory and then a third fortune when he returned to the bakery business.

That development was fuelled in part by the existence of new machinery and improved transport such as the 20th century invention of the bread-slicing machine in Battle Creek, Michigan in the USA and the ever decreasing cost of motor transport making it economically viable to deliver bread over a wide area from a single source.

It was part of this great change in the baking industry which led to the establishment of Orpington's Tip Top Bakery.

The original plot for the Tip Top Bakery of approximately four and a half acres was purchased by Allied Bakeries on the eve of the second world war in 1938 for just £6,000.

Top: *Putting the finishing touches to iced cakes.*
Above: *An early aerial view of the Tip Top factory.*

George's son Willard Garfield Weston was a slice off the same loaf. After having been almost driven out of business by the Wall Street crash of 1929 he scraped together enough money to take his family back to its roots in England to begin all over again.

The first thing Garfield Weston did was introduce British customers to Ryvita. By 1951 he had accumulated more than enough wealth to buy Fortnum & Mason.

But in 1938 the Fortnum & Mason purchase was still in the future and the Tip Top bakery was Weston's priority. Whilst the plot was near to the then quite new 'Arterial Road' it was situated in a very rural area: to the West it was virtually open land, mainly raspberry and strawberry fields through to the railway line.

The bakery was completed in 1939 and was amongst the first factories in the area. Gradually further plots were purchased, factories erected at Sevenoaks Way/Cray Avenue became Orpington Industrial estate. At the time the bakery was built Orpington itself was still little more than a village with a large amount of open land and farmland around although housing estates were beginning to appear and there was obviously a great sales potential for bread.

The bakery opened during the latter part of 1939 for the production of bread only with two plants operating. Cake production began in 1940/41.

It was not the most auspicious moment to open a new bakery. The winds of war were blowing fiercely from the continent. Even as the plant opened Prime Minister Neville Chamberlain's dreadful words must have cast a pall of gloom over what should have been a time for celebration. We were at war with Germany.

For almost a year little happened, Dunkirk came and went. Then came the Battle of Britain with Hurricanes and Spitfires fighting it out with Messerschmits and Heinkels over the South of England. Workers at the Tip Top bakery were there to witness what Churchill called the finest hour in our island history.

Yet for those working in the bread industry came an all too acute awareness of other problems. Our gallant fighter pilots may have won the battle of the air but the battle for the sea and the Atlantic shipping lanes was far from won. Disrupted supplies of flour and the rationing of basic foodstuffs soon told their own sorry tale.

Above right: An advert for Sunblest from the 1950s.
Right: A young Margaret Thatcher, MP, meeting a bread salesman. Deliveries were still made by horse and cart until the late 1960s.

Wheat for bread came mostly from the North American continent. Hitler intended to starve the British into submission by sinking grain ships, and

A simple sailor, lowly born,
Unlettered and unknown,
Who toils for bread from early morn
Till half the night has flown.

Sunblest bread – well worth toiling for . . .

The sign of good bread

Sunblest

Fresh to the last slice

any other merchant shipping which carried supplies for Britain. In the following years packs of German U Boats haunted the sea lanes of the Atlantic scouring the waves for unprotected merchant vessels. And those U Boats were at first only too successful. Government reports of the period expressed deep concern that the volume of grain stored in Britain was rapidly diminishing and might at any point fall below safe levels. Those working at the Tip Top bakery knew perfectly well what the situation was but, for fear of causing alarm to relatives and friends, kept their mouths shut and their fingers crossed.

In the end the supply problem was eased if not solved. The introduction of the convoy system eventually turned the tide with far fewer vessels being lost to the U Boat wolf packs. Britain and its bread hungry citizens lived to fight their way to victory over the Nazi terror.

During the war years pigs were kept on land at the rear of the bakery and fed on waste bread. An

executive club was formed to manage the welfare of the animals and when the pigs were slaughtered the members of the club each had a joint of meat to take home.

The outbreak of war had meant other changes too. Sliced bread for example was no longer available, and Tip Top's slicing machine stood idle. Similarly attractive wrappers for bread had been designed but were not destined to appear until the 'period of austerity' ended many years after the war's end.

Eventually, however, once again fleets of lorries loaded with sacks of flour fresh from the granaries of the United Kingdom, the USA and the rest of the world would become a common sight turning off the Orpington by-pass and heading for the Tip Top bakery.

The bulk of bread is made from wheat obtained from Canada, the USA and

Meet a great new TV star

Sunblest

WHITE SLICED BREAD

Now! Sunblest back on TV... in a brand new wrap

Sunblest launch new national T.V campaign this October. 275 – 15 and 30 second spots in just 4 weeks. Audience: at least 97% of all housewives. Watch out for it. And the rush that follows.

Now Sunblest has a new wrap. And it's a real stand-out! In recent consumer tests the new wrap got twice the rating of other leading brands. Colour coded to show different slicings, wholemeal varieties.

Sunblest - the sign of good sales

Above: *A Sunblest advert from 1965.*
Below: *A Bakery Exhibition in the 1950s.*

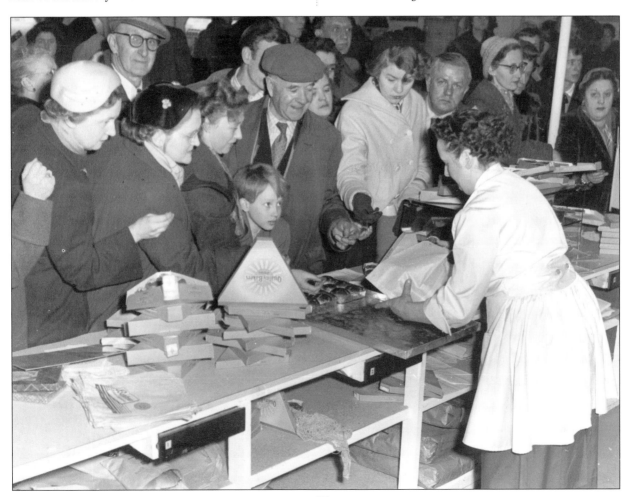

Australia. Little English wheat goes to bread.

From the lorries the sacks were elevated into the Flour Loft waiting their turn there to be made into bread. The flour was then tipped into a hopper to pass through a sieving machine which automatically removed any impurities. The bags in those pre-tanker days were later completely emptied of flour by a suction machine before being returned to the millers.

The preliminary stages of bread making took place in the Dough Room, a large air-conditioned, spotlessly clean place with shiny machines tended by white clad workers. The room's temperature and humidity was controlled by the Dough Room staff to ensure that the atmosphere was kept at the optimum for dough-making.

In the dough-making machine 1,000 lbs of dough could be made at one time; the then ultra-modern machine took around four minutes to achieve what would previ-ously have taken four or five times as long. Flour was automatically weighed before being fed into the mixer and other ingredients such as yeast, salt and water as well as malts and fats were added at the same time. At the press of a button the process began until at the touch of another button the machine gave an almighty heave depositing the mixed dough into a waiting bowl.

What followed next was a period of fermentation. One mix would fill only half a bowl but during fermentation the dough gradually rose until it was completely filled.

The matured dough then passed to a weighing and dividing machine, automatically separating the dough into compact portions of equal and predetermined weight. Once the portions were divided they passed on to the first 'hander-up' where they were rolled and moulded. Then a further period of fermentation was allowed, helped by passing the portions of dough along a moving belt and into the first 'prover', a machine which simply raised the dough's temperature slightly so stimulating further fermentation.

After a short period in the 'prover' the dough passed to one of a number of moulders according to the shape of the loaf required, and was rolled and moulded into its final shape before being placed in a baking tin shaped to produce the required loaf.

After a period of further fermentation in a final 'prover' the dough was fully mature and ready to proceed to the ovens.

The Tip Top ovens were 9 feet wide and 75 feet long. The loaves passed through the ovens on continuous travelling plates with the process being carefully observed by means of inspection windows set throughout the ovens' length. After baking the hot crisp loaves were emptied from their tins by hand and loaded onto the bread cooler - an even larger piece of equipment than the ovens - carrying the loaves on travelling trays allowing them to cool naturally.

Above: Sunblest adverts from the 1970s.
Top: A Tip Top shop in the 1970s.

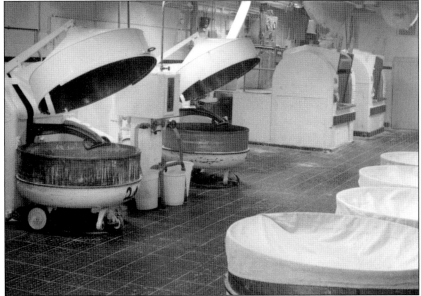

At the end of their journey through the bakery loaves were taken through into the dispatch department where Tip Top's fleets of red and maroon lorries, vans and electric wagons and their drivers waited to deliver bread to shops and, eventually, customers' door steps.

Initially three wholesale routes had been operated but the greater proportion of sales was retail i.e. door to door sales. The main means of transporting the bread on retail routes was by hand barrow, some with electrically operated vehicles. Depots operated at Eltham and Dartford and there horse

Above: *The dough mixing room in the 1960s.*
Top: *The Tip Top factory in the early 1980s.*

drawn transport was used; there were also three retail shops.

During the passing years the company acquired many more retail shops in addition to increasing the number of wholesale and retail routes and operating mobile shops. Numerous alterations were made to the bakery and in 1966 additional adjoining land was purchased - some three quarters of an acre - at a cost of £32,000 to allow for building extensions.

By 1970 the company was operating 114 retail shops, plus retail and wholesale routes and producing bread, rolls and cakes. At that time it was decided to alter the format of the company. A number of the retail shops were transferred to associated shop operating companies. In 1971 the remainder of the shops were transferred or closed and Tip Top ceased to operate shops completely. At the same time the confectionery bakery was closed and there followed a rationalisation programme. Tip Top then became a wholesale bread producing company with just a few retail routes which were gradually phased out.

In 1972/73 further land was purchased - approximately one and a half acres - at a cost of £220,000 again to allow for necessary extensions to the premises and installation of new plant.

In the early 1970s new 18 and 15 sack bread plants were installed and these have since had extensive refurbishment and additions. One of the major changes to occur since the installation of those plants has been the bagging of bread as opposed to the previous over-wrapping. This required a complete new system and equipment for bagging, tying and coding the products. A further innovation in the 1980s was the demand by large multiples for own-label wrapping.

The site now occupied by Tip Top is almost seven acres in size and the company has almost 100 vehicles serving over 80 wholesale routes and five night dairies. The majority of the routes giving daily deliveries to supermarkets, smaller shops, dairies, cafes, hospitals, homes etc. are in the London area covering the City and West End and the London Boroughs south of the Thames. They also operate in north west Kent and in the border towns of Surrey.

In the mid 1980s there was an extensive works programme involving the installation of a new flour and ingredient handling plant; a new 7,000 loaves per hour bread plant and all ancillary equipment and the up-dating and replacement of packaging equipment. The majority of work was

Right: An aerial view of the factory in the early 1980s.
Below: A float taking part in Orpington Carnival.

completed at the end of 1987 making Tip Top one of the largest and most modern bakeries in the United Kingdom enabling it to give an even better service to its customers in the provision of fresh daily products.

During 1995 Tip Top made news headlines delivering medicines. Life saving medicines, baby food and clothing were delivered to British nurses in Bosnia thanks to the efforts of the Metropolitan Police and actor Peter Ellis - Chief Superintendent Brownlow in the soap The Bill. Trucks carrying items such as sterilising equipment left Hendon Police College in April 1995. Making the journey in a Tip Top bakery truck were Inspector Anthony Moor, a retired Met officer, Eric Freeman and Peter Ellis. Tip Top general manager Paul Longley agreed to donate the loan of a bread lorry, petrol and malt loaves to the appeal.

loaves, cobs, whole-meals and any number of other bread products which can only be satisfied by production on a large scale.

Inexorably, step by step, the history of baking and bread making has led directly from that first stone-ground fire-baked loaf to the modern baking industry - and to the Tip Top Bakery - now renamed Allied Bakeries Orpington, with one of the largest bread producing plants in the country which produces the country's leading bread brand of Kingsmill.

Above left: Breadmaking in the 21st century.
Below: The Allied Bakeries factory.

Nor was that the last lorry loan: when Baptist minister the Reverend Clive Doubleday, pastor of Provost Road Baptist Church, decided to concentrate on overseas missionary and humanitarian work, Allied Bakeries' Tip Top bakery was right behind him when he decided to take 2,000 boxes of aid to Pristina in Kosovo. The boxes contained clothing, blankets and toiletries donated by local churches, schools and residents. Staff at the Tip Top bakery lent Rev Doubleday and fellow driver Derek Lee-Philpot a lorry for the 3,200 mile journey. Bread is of course mentioned many times in the Bible.

Bread is the most basic of our foodstuffs; a prime commodity. No matter what ups and downs of the economy, no matter what changes in fashion occur, no matter what fads for fancy food come and go bread will remain with us forever, consumer demand persisting no matter how demand for other products may fall and rise.

'Let them eat cake' was Marie Antoinette's supposed response to the news that French peasants were rioting because of a shortage of bread. She may not have really said that, but the very idea expressed as political propaganda by the French revolutionaries demonstrated just how important bread is in our lives.

When our far distant ancestors first ground wild grass seeds and formed the resultant flour into a paste to make the first bread they could not have imagined the consequences of their action. From those primitive beginnings have come seas of Canadian prairie land covered with swaying wheat stalks, huge grain ships, sailing across the oceans to enormous silos in docks across the world. The invention of baking led to the demand for sliced

This grand victory procession took place at Coney Hall on May 19th 1945, a sign that although May 8th had been official VE (Victory in Europe) Day, celebrations continued in the weeks that followed. Rumours of the imminent end of the war had circulated freely in early May and the atmosphere was full of waiting. Then, on the evening of May 7th 1945, came the announcement of Germany's surrender, and the rejoicing began. There was dancing on the streets, singing, flag-waving, bonfires and the pealing of church bells. Buildings such as the Town Hall in Beckenham, and many others, were floodlit after dark, a nice contrast to the blackout of not so long before. The Coney Hall celebration, a little later, featured no less than 760 children, and as the photograph shows, Britain's allies were not forgotten, particularly the USA. The procession was followed by tea at the Coney Hall and at Coney Hill Free Church hall. The highlight of the later variety entertainment at Wickham Common School was the appearance of a huge three-tiered iced cake which required three men to carry it in. It was big enough for every child to have a piece, and had been made by Mrs Simmonds of Sylvan Way.

Events & occasions

Above: Smiling faces all round as this cheerful group poses for the camera before getting on with the party. This celebration for the residents of Meadow Road, Shortlands, was held in August 1945, to mark the defeat and surrender of Japan. Almost six years of bitter conflict was finally at an end! The soldiers' huts on the Meadow Road site were loaned to the residents for the day, and about 60 children, including some from Beckenham Lane, were given a wonderful time. Long tables were laid out with party fare inside one of the big huts, and the centrepiece Victory Cake was the work of Mrs Colley. Most of the fun took place outdoors, however, with children's races on the nearby golf course, and a Men v Women tug-of-war. A bonfire and fireworks rounded off a memorable day for the children, and as well as the various prizes awarded, each child received a 2s 6d National Savings stamp. It was probably difficult to get the children off to bed, no matter how tired they were, but this having been achieved there was dancing for the adults to Cox's Band.

Both pages: Two things for certain emerge from this sequence of photographs taken along Beckenham High Street on Coronation day in 1953 - firstly that it was not high summer weather; secondly that this did not deter the crowds from gathering to make the most of a momentous event. Plenty of effort had been expended in mounting the patriotic street decorations, and despite the cold and damp weather, young and old gathered in force on the afternoon of June 2nd 1953 to celebrate the Coronation of Queen Elizabeth II. It was believed that this was the first time that Beckenham High Street had been completely closed to traffic. This was a landmark event in British life, and there is no doubt that those who experienced it will have some vivid memory of it. Perhaps it might be a recollection of receiving a Coronation mug at school. How many of those have survived? Above all, many people remember watching the morning ceremony on television, often in a church hall or a municipal building, for not many could claim ownership of a television then. This was the first time that people could share a national event collectively, through the medium of television, and although the screens were small and the pictures were in grainy black and white, it proved to be an unforgettable experience.

The afternoon was given over to local celebrations of all kinds, which continued for several days, and wherever possible the weather was braved so that the children could enjoy their street parties. The pictured scenes on Beckenham High Street all formed part of the Coronation Fair, opened by the Mayor, Alderman WJ Sampson. Accompanied by his wife, he had been transported in style from the Town Hall in a vintage 1901 De Dion car. After the opening ceremony, children of the Grove Dancing and Dramatic Club performed a floral dance along the length of the High Street. All the fun of the fair was enjoyed for the rest of the day, with traditional sideshows such as Punch and Judy alongside more unusual attractions such as the 'unrideable horse' and the 'topsy-turvy boat'. A continuous cavalcade of music and dancing accompanied the festivities, including maypole dancing and entertainment provided by the Beckenham Choir, the Ravensbourne Morris men and various bands.

Memories of BROMLEY

The newly crowned monarch's broadcast to the nation, at 9pm, was relayed along the High Street through a tannoy system, and the Mayor led the cheers for Her Majesty. All around the Bromley district a colourful and varied range of events took place through which people showed both their patriotism and their optimism for the future. The crowning of a new young queen seemed to represent a step forward, a clean break with the dreary post-war days of rationing and austerity. A touch of colour and pageantry was the tonic that the nation needed. The new Elizabethan Age had dawned, and this new spirit seemed to be summed up in that jaunty little piece of music that was constantly played on the radio - 'Elizabethan Serenade'. Many of the local celebrations

consciously made the link with the reign of the first Elizabeth. For example, Beckenham and West Wickham Townswomen's Guilds put on an exhibition at the Public Hall, Beckenham, entitled 'The Two Elizabeths'. Also, amidst the 100 stands set up by Bromley Chamber of Commerce in a giant marquee on Queens Mead was a one ton, slowly rotating 'world', 12 feet in diameter. Its theme was Elizabethan enterprise, and the globe was surmounted by a model of the 'Golden Hind', Drake's famous ship.

The Chamber of Commerce's marquee formed part of an ambitious eight day 'Coronade' at Queens Mead. By the fifth day it had attracted 15,000 visitors, and 5,000 of these had come on Wednesday, the day after the Coronation, when the Carnival procession had wound its

way through Bromley's streets to Queens Mead. Although once again it was miserably cold that evening, it did not deter the thousands who lined the streets to cheer the decorated tableaux depicting Britain's achievements 'From Elizabeth to Elizabeth'. The Carnival procession was led by the Bromley Home Guard Band, and five floats were needed to accommodate all the May Queens of Bromley, with their attendants. One of the most spectacular events of the previous evening had been the lighting of Keston's monster 30 feet high beacon (one of 1,400 throughout Britain) by Bromley's Mayor, Councillor Leighton L Irwin.

Both pages: War Weapons Week in February 1941 is the focus of these two photographs. A grand march past outside the Town Hall on Tweedy Road has attracted plenty of spectators, including a few who have taken time off from their duties inside to come and have a grandstand view at the windows. Nevertheless there is a reminder in the first photograph *(left)* that living in wartime Bromley involved more than enjoying parades, for the entry to the air-raid shelter on the pavement is plain to see. The gentleman taking the salute, with his hand raised, was Brigadier James Whitehead and the second photograph *(above)* shows a close-up of the same occasion, with the Brigadier standing third from left. In between the Mayor's macebearer and Brigadier Whitehead stands Colonel Chamberlain, whilst the Mayor of Bromley himself is just to the right of the Brigadier, but slightly obscured by him. More dignitaries and their wives stand in the patriotically decorated dais at the rear - overall a colourful and impressive occasion. Events such as War Weapons Week had a number of purposes, including those of fostering community effort and raising morale,

but the primary aim was to raise money. 'Total war' for Britain meant pouring almost all her resources into defeating the enemy on land, at sea and in the air. Enormous quantities of materials were needed whilst the opportunities to earn money by trade were badly dislocated. The government had to raise as much money as it could from its own people. Hence a constant stream of government leaflets urged people to be patriotic and buy War Bonds or other forms of National Savings. For War Weapons Week the figures were:- Beckenham £604,000, Bromley £450,000, Orpington £259,000 and Penge £90,000. The major campaign of 1942 was Warship Week during which Bromley and Beckenham each raised £600,000. Bromley 'adopted' the battleship, 'HMS Broke', whilst Beckenham 'adopted' the destroyer, 'HMS Sikh'. The RAF got its turn in 1943 with Wings for Victory, and Bromley raised enough money to pay for 8 Lancaster bombers, 16 Typhoon fighters and 14 Spitfires. By the time of Salute the Soldier Week, in 1944, Beckenham had already raised a staggering £2.5 million for National Savings - with more to come!

ot just one May Queen, but a whole line of them, with their young attendants, makes for a colourful occasion at Hayes in 1936. May Queens and spring festivities are deeply rooted in our history, often associated with maypole dancing and fairs. There is no doubt that something of this sort must have gone on in Hayes in medieval times, but the modern version, as pictured here, was of relatively recent origin. It was devised in 1913 by Mr Deedy, a folklore enthusiast, to be held annually on the second Saturday in May. A famous local personality always headed the

procession in the 1920s, Mr Frank Price. He was a shepherd with the well-known Hambro family for 38 years, and Mr Price always cut a distinctive figure in his shepherd's smock. The annual event at Hayes is of still of more than purely local importance, for many areas elect their own May Queens and send them to Hayes, where the May Queen of London is crowned. No doubt this was the grand event captured by the photographer in 1936, and the theme of the leading queen and her retinue is that of roses. The bombs of World War II failed to put a stop to these popular festivities.

Both pages: Fire-engines fill the street, hosepipes snake everywhere and a large crowd watches as the Harrison Gibson furniture store goes up in flames in these two dramatic photographs from February 1968. No sooner had the New Year sales ended (a three-piece suite for £80!) than £65,000 worth of stock was destroyed in what was at the time Bromley's worst peacetime blaze. Not only this, but the Harrison Gibson enterprise, a long-established one in Bromley, had now been badly hit three times in 27 years. An air-raid in 1941 had caused thousands of pounds worth of damage to the firm's Ringers Road warehouse and in 1945, a few weeks after the end of the war, a fire had badly damaged the soft furnishings department. The blaze of February 1968 began at two-thirty in the afternoon on the second floor, and by three o'clock flames were engulfing the upper floors. Luckily, staff and customers all got out safely, and it was left to the firefighters to do what they could. Soon 100 firemen from 25 fire appliances were engaged in a desperate battle not so much to save Harrison Gibson's as to try and stop the fire spreading to other premises along High Street. The

pictures give some flavour of the scene as shoppers stood rooted to the spot to watch firemen on their escape ladders directing jets of water into the inferno as 20 feet long tongues of flame came leaping towards them. The dense smoke made respirators necessary and one fireman suffered head injuries as the roof collapsed. Meanwhile the police had sealed off the area to traffic, but not before one bewildered lorry driver, with a delivery of furniture for the store, on asking for directions had been told, 'Straight down the High Street. You can't miss it - it's on fire!' At last the heroic firemen managed to battle their way into the building where they unleashed thousands of gallons of water. This, along with the presence of some stout steel doors, prevented the flames roaring through the subway to the Harrison Gibson store on Ringers Road. Surrounding businesses were also saved, although there was some slight damage to Wolfe and Hollander's warehouse. Nevertheless the danger of a collapse of Harrison and Gibson's badly damaged 60 feet high walls meant the evacuation of nearby homes and businesses until a demolition team could move in, ruin for quite a while after and even the ruin caught fire!

Above: The local MP, Sir Edward Campbell, standing at far right, leads the applause as a parade along Tweedy Road on September 13th 1941 opens the Salvage Drive for Victory week in Bromley. It was to be followed by competitions, sports events, entertainments and more parades during the next few days. That the collection of salvage for recycling was given a special campaign week of its own is an indicator of its importance to the British war effort. The parades were not just an entertainment. Displays of weapons and vehicles, such as the one pictured in the lead, were a pointed reminder that collecting scrap metal would enable many more to be manufactured. A lighter note could be struck, of course, and in 1943 the Women's Voluntary Service (WVS) organised a Domestic Front exhibition at the Bromley Central Library, and one of the stalls exhibited toys made from salvaged materials. The WVS was tremendously active in this field, organising salvage collections constantly. Waste paper drives, involving donations of books, were a popular theme. The Mayor, Councillor H Lynch Watson, put down the first book to start the Mile of Books, all for recycling, in July 1942 - a 'mile' which ultimately stretched almost two miles. Other 'miles' were to follow in 1944.

Right: 'Water, water everywhere..' was the headline of the 'Bromley and Kentish Times' after a weekend deluge in September 1968 produced scenes like this all around the district. The forlorn sight of marooned and abandoned cars was an all too common one, and although it was Courage beer that was being advertised at The Lord Holmesdale, it was this quality which had to be shown by thousands of householders facing floodwater and electricity cuts. A downpour of 48 hours proved too much for the River Ravensbourne and the local drains, the result being an unstoppable tide of water in some areas. Some families had to retreat upstairs, Sunday lunch forgotten, as several feet of water swirled in the streets below them. Firemen and police had to use boats for rescue work in areas such as Lower Camden and Southend Lane. Water cascading down hillsides and railway embankments added to the problem. An estimated five inches of rain fell on that September weekend, but the true amount could not be recorded because the Parks Department's rain gauge was soon under two feet of water! Showing true British 'bulldog spirit', however, the regulars at the Shortlands Tavern carried on drinking, and perhaps the same was going on at the The Lord Holmesdale.

On the move

A 1968 shot of the top of Station Approach, Hayes, shows a fine collection of some of the cars of that era, not least the Mini van, the Morris Minor and the famous 'half-timbered' Morris Traveller. No doubt the sight arouses some fond recollections in the memories of some readers. Although there is a very urban feel to this scene, only 35 years earlier, in 1933, the station and the New Inn would have been the only buildings present. The New Inn was originally a pub that had been built close to the station, around 1900, to attract the passing trade.

Hayes Station had been opened in in 1882. The scheme was the brainchild of Everard Hambro, a wealthy banker who lived at the mansion of Hayes Place, the original home of Pitt the Younger. The pub was to go through many transformations. In 1935 it was demolished to make way for a stylish new roadhouse. However, at the height of the Battle of Britain, September 15th 1940, a bomb devastated the New Inn, killing the head waiter and also the husband of a waitress. The New Inn was not to reopen until 1962, and was revamped internally in the 1980s.

Below centre: Change and the High Street have gone hand-in-hand over the centuries. The same can be said of Market Square, which this view of around 1960 captures in the background, and one of the fundamental factors in change has been the growth in traffic of various sorts. Traditionally the home of a market on Thursdays, Market Square was once a busy scene of stalls spreading around the buildings in haphazard fashion. However, by the eighteenth century, Bromley had become an important part of the coaching trade. As early as 1832 buildings were demolished in Market Square to allow easier passage of coaches. Traffic problems of a different kind were arising by the 1920s - those posed by the motor-car. A central block that had housed Paynes the jewellers was demolished, along with the Victorian Town Hall, and in 1932 the market was moved to its present position near Bromley North Station. The rehousing of Paynes in the building that faces the camera in the background meant that its link with Market Square continued, and still does. The sight of the Morris Minor speeding up High Street around 1960 symbolises the beginning of even greater problems, associated with the rise of mass car ownership, leading ultimately to the pedestrianisation of the area.

Bottom: The sight of the sign 'Quad Green Shield' is enough to whisk anyone back to the 1960s and 1970s. Such an offer was bound to lure a few extra customers to the petrol pumps, but in the last week of May 1969 there was enough going on at the Victory Motor Company (Masons Hill, Bromley) to pull in the crowds without the offer of extra green shield stamps. The date marked the 50th anniversary of continuous Ford service at Masons Hill. Amongst the attractions on display to commemorate the golden jubilee were a Model 'T' fire engine of 1906, a Ford V8 Pilot and an American Lincoln Continental. Performance cars on view included Graham Hill's 1968 World Championship Lotus Formula One car. The enthusiasts must have loved it! More realistically, they would have been able to browse under the Used Car Canopy, seen to the far left, and known locally as the 'Canopy of Light'. A 1965 Ford Corsair, for example cost £485. Bromley acquired a main dealership link with Ford in 1919, when the franchise was granted to Soans and Dunn, a local family business. New owners changed the name to Victory (Ford) in 1964, and modernisation of the showrooms, service department and parts department followed in 1964. The site is now owned by Bristol Street Motors.

Left: Strange hooded creatures arrived on the streets of Central Bromley in October 1968, and the removal of the hoods announced the fact that parking meters had arrived. Parking meters were never the most popular innovations amongst motorists and traders, especially when accompanied by the dreaded traffic warden, and there was the predictable furore when they were introduced into Bromley. Particularly incensed were the Market Square traders, who complained that the meters made the loading and unloading of goods difficult, and at peak times of the day impossible beacause of prohibitions. The regional organiser of Oxfam was less than enchanted at a meter being placed outside the premises on Elmfield Road, fearing that its presence would deter people from bringing gifts. There was a feeling amongst shopkeepers that customers might well go elsewhere, to places such as Hayes and West Wickham. The Borough Engineer, Mr B T Collins, defended the introduction of parking meters as an alternative to the more stringent restrictions that might have been introduced to cope with growing traffic congestion. Meters soon became familiar enough, along with yellow lines, restricted zones and a degree of pedestrianisation in most town centres.

Above: The workmen on the left have got a wonderful view of High Street when they can take a moment off to enjoy it. What they see, of course, is a sight that has been an all too common one over the years - disruption of traffic. Whether or not this was called a 'contra-flow system' in the 1930s, it amounted to the same thing. With regard to the townscape, some interesting features are visible, although most of the shop names would be unfamiliar to modern ears, the main exception being what was Dolcis, this now being the main entrance to the Glades Shopping Centre, up the street to the right. Immediately above Dolcis, the spire of the Methodist Church, opened in 1875, dominates the skyline. The shop that later went on down High Street, below the church, fortunately did not destroy the fine buildings, and the workmen were in a position to cast a professional eye over the elegant gables and balconies. The substantial building at the top of High Street, on the left, was the Central Library. Below that was Ravensfell, with its high roof and tall chimney, the upper floors of which have survived the huge changes which have since transformed the Central Library area.

At the shops

All the bustle and activity of a good old-fashioned street market comes across in this shot of Market Square. Fruit, fish, flowers amd hanging poultry are just a few of the items on view, along with indispensable accessories such as weighing scales and handcarts. Markets in most towns have a long history, and Bromley is no exception. The Bishop of Rochester, as Lord of the Manor, was granted a charter to hold a Tuesday market in 1205, changing to Thursday in 1447, and a second charter was granted by King Henry VI in 1447. The date of this particular photograph is uncertain, but the ladies' hat styles in the foreground suggest the 1920s. The posters on the right, advertising the Grand Theatre and the 'The People' newspaper, have their interest, but the small poster to the left of these mentions Remembrance Day, and invites people to 'Wear a Flanders Poppy'. The terrible events of World War I, which had ended in 1918, would have been close enough to give real meaning to Poppy Day for this throng in Market Square. The very familiar name of EW Payne, jewellers, is visible in the background, a firm which has traded in Market Square since 1910, having originally taken over the premises of the old Forester Inn.

A busy and active commercial life has long been a feature of Bromley High Street, and this 1935 view sees a range of shops and stores stretching as far as the Central Library in the background. The vehicles have a definitely 1930s look about them, not least the bus in the distance with its rear entry steps to the upper deck. If the vehicles are unfamiliar to the modern eye, so are the shop names for the most part, although the Fifty Shillings Tailor was a well-known chain of shops at the time. One name that would not be unknown to some readers, however, is that of Harrison Gibson Ltd, at far left. Specialising in house furnishings, this firm was prominent in the town for many years, although it met with a number of setbacks. The Ringers Road warehouse suffered a direct hit in a 1941 air-raid, with the loss of a large amount of stock. Shortly after the war, a fire in the High Street soft furnishings department did serious damage. Finally, in 1968 virtually on the eve of a take-over by the Army and Navy Stores, a spectacular blaze gutted Harrison Gibson's High Street store, in spite of the attentions of over 100 firemen.

Fruit, flowers and veg seem to be the theme at the top end of Market Square in a scene that dates back to the 1920s. And if it appears to be congested in the foreground, it only gets worse approaching the impressive landmark building of David Greig - Tea and Provisions. The other names on view - Curwoods, W Dell, Elanel, Winton's - all seem very unfamiliar now, but the firm of Greig was trading in meat and groceries until relatively modern times. The inscription 'David Greig 1912' may still be seen on the upper reaches of that grand white facade. The weekly Bromley market has been held traditionally on Thursdays since 1447. The right to do this would have been lost if one single market day had been missed, and so it became essential for many years to set up one stall for a short time (at least one hour) if Christmas Day happened to fall on a Thursday. The old market characters were often colourful individuals, but life could be precarious for the traders in the early years of the twentieth century. Some had to take their families into the workhouse at Farnborough in winter, when trade was poor. In 1932 the market was moved to its present site by Bromley North station.

Above: The little group of people on the corner of High Street and Church Road would be very familiar with the names of the shops and businesses around them in 1961. Perhaps one or two of them had dropped in for a quick snack at Gwen's Pantry, next door to John Hood, Dyers and Cleaners. Also, no matter how businesses come and go, it is a fair bet that they felt there was something of permanence about the presence of the Midland Bank and the store of F Medhurst, just across the road. However, since that time the bank has undergone an identity change, and the name of Medhurst too has disappeared, a name which seemed to be part of the very commercial fabric of Bromley in 1961. The firm was founded by Fred Medhurst, who began as a general draper in 1879 with three small shops on High Street. Such was Fred's success that he soon began to expand into adjacent property, the most famous of which came to be number 47 High Street. This was the china shop of Mr Joseph Wells, and the birthplace of HG Wells. It was taken over by Fred Medhurst in 1887. There was continued expansion in the next century, and although the Church Road entrance on the photograph looks modest enough, it was awaiting its inclusion in the 1959 to 1962 modernisation programme that the store was carrying out along High Street. Nevertheless by 1980 the Medhurst name had been replaced by that of Allders.

Above right: The linking of the words 'draper' and 'Bromley' seems instantly to conjure up thoughts of HG Wells, one of the most famous draper's apprentices in history. However, although born at 47 High Street, Wells' apprenticeship was on the south coast, and he did not learn the trade under the care of Frederick William Orton, 'the popular draper', of 146 High Street. In 1935 Bromley High Street abounded with a rich and varied mixture of small businesses and shops, and on this photograph the eye is most caught by Mrs Dean's fruit and veg shop, thrusting itself outwards across the pavement. The gentleman doing the serving is being kept pretty busy in this traditional style of retailing, reminiscent of the open market. Even with all the huge changes that have transformed retailing in recent years, echoes of old street trading still exist in the shape of the farmers market in the pedestrianised area of the High Street, 'cheek by jowl' with the modern Glades Shopping Centre. It was in 1935, the date of this photograph, that Wilson's Cafe opened at 88 High Street, soon to become famous for a rich aroma of roasting coffee permeating the atmosphere, perhaps as far as Mrs Dean's shop.

Below: Medhursts is all aglow in 1968 as the Christmas illuminations brighten the darkness. The Christmas display had been a feature at Medhursts since 1960, the time at which the new building, running from numbers 186 to 192 High Street, had been constructed. Along with the rebuilding had been expansion, followed by a completely new frontage in 1964. Medhursts had come a long way since Fred Medhurst set up his humble drapery business at High Street in 1879. Joined by other members of the family, Fred continued a process of expansion and rebuilding right up to his death in the mid-1930s, making the business a household name in Bromley. 'Living in' for some of the staff, for example milliners and dressmakers, lasted until 1939, and a full apprenticeship scheme continued until this date. A 1935 price list makes for interesting reading, with a box of six coloured woven handkerchiefs for two shillings (10p) and a Morocco leather

Cocktail Bag for £1. Fred Medhurst would no doubt have been proud of what he had begun if he had been able to see the modern store of 1968. However his great-nephew, John Taylor-Medhurst, felt impelled by the business pressures of the day to sell the family firm in 1969. The name Medhursts was retained, although it became part of a large chain, and the centenary was celebrated in 1979 amidst another big rebuilding programme. Medhursts became Allders in 1980, although the old name is still visible, carved high up on the stonework.

Bottom: The sign of the Star and Garter public house holds a prominent position, unfortunately much of its very distinctive architecture is obscured in this view along Bromley High Street. The photographer caught the High Street in a busy mood around 1970, and one of the long term survivors of this shot has been the Odeon. It was opened in 1936, during the heyday of the construction of purpose-built cinemas, with a seating capacity of 1492. The first film shown was 'Educated Evans'. The entrepreneur Oscar Deutsch established a chain of around 300 Odeon cinemas in the 1930s. The 'house-style' was a streamlined look, with large areas of cream tiling and that distinctive gold and red geometric lettering of 'Odeon'. Across the street the Astor was not to fare as well as the Odeon. Originally opened as the Palais de Luxe, seating 731, it had very mixed fortunes. It was closed in 1940 and became a store for the Ministry of Food. Having been refurbished the Palais reopened in 1949, being renamed the Pullman in 1954. Another change in 1963 saw the Astor emerge, but it was to close as a cinema in 1977 in order to accommodate the then relentless march of bingo and has since disappeared.

Making a living

It would be interesting to know where the photographer was standing, possibly in a precarious position, but the result was an impressive one of workmen silhouetted against the sky. Even more precarious is the position of the men themselves, who appear to be finding only the slenderest of footholds as they wield their pickaxes. There does not appear to be much of a margin of error, and a modern safety inspector would be aghast. Also there is no sign of a safety helmet, just the traditional flat caps. However, this was 1931, when helmets were unheard of outside the pits. It was also a time, just two years after the American Wall Street Crash and the resultant world-wide depression, when unemployment was rampant. Men were glad of jobs, and perhaps did not argue too much about safety matters. The job in hand was the demolition of Bromley House in High Street, to make way for new buildings. It had formerly been the residence of several prominent local people, but over the previous few years it had housed the Inland Revenue office. In that case perhaps the workers were volunteers!

Mrs Wrathall of Glenview Road, Bromley, was certainly doing her bit for the war effort in this scene captured in 1940. Her handcart is packed with goodies, especially the two sacks which are bulging with paper, jars and cans. With shortages of all kinds being imposed by the sinking of merchant ships by German U-boats, it was important for Britain to be as self-sufficient as possible. One way was for people to grow as much of their own food as possible, and so began the Dig for Victory campaign. By April 1940 Bromley had 67 acres of allotments compared to the 37 acres of pre-war days. Salvage was considered just as crucial, for recycling purposes, and in 1940 Bromley collected 450 tons of waste paper and 410 tons of metal. Bones and jam jars were not overlooked either. In terms of equipping the armed services, scrap metal was the most important salvage item. The old tram lines at Penge were dug up and the demolition of the Crystal Palace water towers produced around 1,600 tons of scrap metal. Even the railings from parks and schools disappeared - virtually never to return!

Above: No doubt a grand day out is being anticipated by the staff of Dunn's Depository at Widmore Road, Bromley, as they pose for this 1930 photograph. One fully loaded charabanc awaits and everybody has turned out in 'Sunday best'. Day trips then were a good deal rarer than they are today, so much so that an effort was usually made to record the occasion, preserving something to evoke fond recollections in later years. The trippers were employees of a notable firm whose headquarters were to be found in Market Square. Established in 1710, and largely specialising in removals and storage, Dunn's premises were destroyed by fire in 1909. A much larger and very elegant replacement shop in Market Square was built in 1927, but this was to be gutted by German bombs in April 1941. It was in the post-war period, however, that Dunn's would come to the forefront in the field of modern and stylish house furnishings. Geoffrey Dunn was in sole control of the rebuilt shop between 1945 and its closure in 1980. He rapidly moved away from the 'safe', mass-produced lines, and Dunn's was among the first British outlets for Swedish furniture designed by Aalto and Mathsson. Geoffrey Dunn always encouraged the work of up-and-coming designers, potters and weavers. He was a designer too in his own right, and although the firm has now gone, it once stood at the heart of the progressive design movement.

Right: It is difficult to know which is most impressive - the line of Dunn's removal and delivery vans or the grand lines of the Town Hall. This 1929 view along Tweedy Road, catches the Town Hall at a good angle for an appreciation of its qualities. It was designed by R Frank Atkinson and built in 1906 at a cost of £35,000. One of the outstanding features is the cupola set above the imposing entrance porch. If the terms 'tasteful' and 'artistic' can be applied to the Town Hall, Dunn's had also appropriated them for their own business from the evidence on the side of the two vans. There was plenty of justification for this too, because Dunn's built up an enviable reputation in their field in the twentieth century. This family business began in 1710 in the heart of Bromley, the Market Square, its main line for many years being removals, storage and undertaking. The retail side was very small at first, but nevertheless Dunn's prided themselves on being house furnishers, as the vans on the photograph show. It was to be under the inspired leadership of Geoffrey Dunn, who ran the business from 1945 to its closure in 1980, that Dunn's of Bromley became synonymous with all that was best in modern British and international furnishing design. Those who visited Dunn's may well remember the area known as The Pavilion, which contained 'the best of the best' .

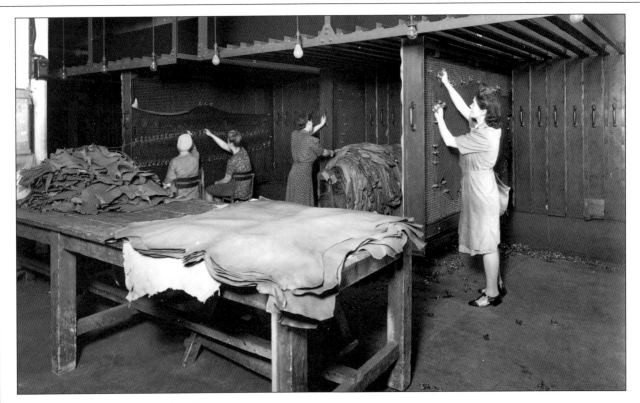

Above: It is not so many years since the Randak tannery of R & A Kohnstamm was still in business on Croydon Road, Elmers End, although this photograph looks as if it dates closer to its opening, in 1934, than its closure. The rough wooden table is covered in leather hides, and the ladies are assisting in the 'toggling' process, by which the surface of the hides was smoothed out. Although the Kohnstamm tannery was built at Elmers End in 1934, the firm had been founded in 1840, and was to the forefront of the leather industry. It continued on this site for several decades after World War II, and in the 1950s the raw material for its leather was coming from crocodiles from Java and East Africa, ostriches from South Africa, sealskins from the Arctic, calfskins and pigskins. Clearly Kohnstamm was engaged in a worldwide operation, but it was only one of many firms which operated in the Elmers End area around the 1950s. Muirhead & Co, for example, was one of the largest in the district, employing over 1,000 workers in the making of precision electrical instruments. Two other notable names were Maybreys, aluminium founders, and Percy Jones (Twinlock Ltd), office equipment manufacturers.

Above right: Graphic images of war on the Home Front form the substance of this photograph of High Street, Penge, between Cottingham Road and Kingsdale Road. The date was September 1st 1941, and the two ladies by the pram must have wondered what sort of a world the child was going to grow up in. At an early stage of the war, some felt that the main danger to civilians was that posed by getting about in the blackout, and the striped lower part of the lamp standard shows one measure that was brought in to help. However, the evidence of the bomb damage, along with the presence of the barrage balloon in the sky, shows where the real danger came from. By January 1941, 600 Penge children had been evacuated to Devon. There were constant bomb incidents in Penge, but local spirit was exemplified by the 'Business As Usual' notices on the Scotch Wool and Hosiery Stores. Worse was to come, however, with the arrival of the flying bombs, or 'doodlebugs', from 1944. Penge was harder hit than any other area by these tremendously destructive weapons. Within one square mile 18 fell, including two on High Street which killed 18 people. At Trenholme Road 12 were killed in July 1944, including several children.

Below: A new style of barricade was being tried out at the junction of North Street and East Street in 1937, but as far as motorists were concerned it meant the same old story - road blocked! As for the workmen, however, digging roads can be thirsty work, and perhaps they were well pleased to be working in such close proximity to the Railway Hotel, opposite Bromley North Station. Perhaps they even appreciated the finer points of the architecture for the Railway Hotel was , and remains, one of those wonderful Victorian buildings that reflected the confidence and vigour of the age. It was built in 1879 for the brewers Nalder and Collyer to serve the passing railway trade, for Bromley North Station had been opened only the year before, in 1878. The green and ochre tiling around the lower section of the Railway Hotel helps to give the building its distinctive appearance. In the joining of

North Street and East Street it is possible to see the makings of a triangle, and indeed West Street completes the shape. The triangular field that once existed before the streets were built was called Cage Field. for it used to house a small prison, with two detention cells, known as the Cage.

Bottom: The Emergency Operations Room at Bromley Town Hall is captured in a fairly relaxed mood in this early 1940s wartime shot. However, both before the war and during the course of the conflict, the Town Hall was the centre of planning and organisation. The first problem was to convince people that war was a probability rather than a possibility, and that the civilian population of Bromley and district would be in the front line of enemy bombing attacks. As early as September 1938 Bromley was divided into seven districts,

each with its own Air Raid Precaution Committee (ARP). By the outbreak of war, in September 1939, Bromley had over 1,000 full time ARP volunteers including air-raid wardens, first-aid workers, drivers and gas decontamination squads. During the frequent German air-raids that later occurred, the Emergency Operations Room was the 'heartbeat' of all the ARP activity, along with directing the police, fire and ambulance services. No doubt the helmets on view were quickly donned when the action began. Training to meet as yet untested emergencies took place regularly. For example on April 12th 1941 'Gas Tests' were held in many local areas, with a simulation of a gas attack, followed by a 'decontamination' exercise. Fortunately the real thing never occurred.

Providing the essential element to the world of printing

Almost unnoticed, printing inks are around us all the time, in shops, buses, trains and in our homes and workplaces. The inks are used in books, newspapers, letterheads, wallpaper, greetings cards, on beer cans, in photo-copying toners and even on printed circuit boards. The list is almost endless.

One of the largest and longest established firms manufac-turing printers' inks is the Coates Lorilleux company based at St Mary Cray.

From its foundation in 1877 the Coates family directed and controlled the affairs of the company for more than a century; at first through the partnership of the original brothers and subse-quently through George's son Maurice, and then for a further thirty years through George's grandson JBM Coates. Dr Henry Coates a nephew of the founders was a director for more than fifty years after having been company secretary from 1922 to 1934.

Lance Coates, JBM Coates' brother, retired in 1975 after 44 years on the board; in the 1930s he had played a crucial part in introducing new technologies and manufacturing methods which provided the base for the company's future expansion through the establishment of branch factories initially in Great Britain and subsequently throughout the world. JBM Coates retired in 1977.

The St Mary Cray site has seen continued growth and expansion since it opened in 1936. Over the years it has seen the manufacture of all types of printing inks including offset, heatset, screen and gravure products.

In more recent years it has estab-lished a 'centre of excellence' for the development of radiation curing products making use of ultra violet light to cure ink. That specialist focus equally applies to the firm's manufac-turing facilities.

It was in 1877 that two young brothers John and George Coates, aged just 20 and 24 set up their own business in London as printers suppliers, chemical merchants and manufacturers of inks and varnishes. Their investment was £100 each, plus a loan of the same amount from two other members of the family.

Three years later business had expanded sufficiently to move into a new production plant at West Ham adjacent to the Lamp Black Factory which provided pigment for Coates' newspaper inks and offset blacks.

Above: Company founders J W Coates, left and his brother George. Below: An ornate company letterhead from the early 1900s. Right: The London office in 1895.

Continued growth allowed the brothers to open a distribution branch in Manchester and by 1888 the business had became a limited company.

One employee of the firm was Mr HC Bolton who in 1890 left the company to establish his own business called Morris & Bolton. Ironically, years later, this became Lorilleux & Bolton and was to play an important role in the future of Coates Brothers.

It was to be John Bernard Maurice Coates, a grandson of George Coates, who had the vision and ability to

Above: The second generation of the family to run the firm, Dr HJ Coates, left and CM Coates. Right: The third generation of the family to be involved with the firm, from left, Lance Coates and his brother John who was Chairman until retirement in 1977. Below: Long service staff pictured in 1927.

turn Coates Brothers into a major force within the printing ink industry; he was a director of the company from 1930; became general manager from 1938 to 1948; was MD and chairman between 1948 to 1970 and from 1956 chairman of the Coates Group of more than 30 companies until his retirement in 1977.

John BM Coates, known as 'Mr John' joined the firm from Cambridge in August 1929 when the firm's office and warehouse were in St Bride's House in Salisbury Square just off Fleet Street. The business then employed just eight staff plus John Coates and his father Maurice Coates.

At that time the factory was run by a manager assisted by a clerk and just fifteen manual workers. The Manchester branch was staffed by a manager, a clerk and a warehouse assistant together with six travellers or reps - two of whom were over 70.

Annual turnover of the business in those days was around £74,000, the great majority of which was sales on the home market.

In 1934 the Lamp Black Factory closed, the Coates Brothers were its last customer. That meant looking elsewhere for supplies of raw materials and coincided with a search for larger and better production facilities.

Two years later a 2.9 acre site was bought in St Mary Cray in Kent. The cost was £3,000 and the West Ham factory was sold for £11,500 which provided the funds to build and equip a modern factory which opened in 1937.

Between 1934 and 1936 the firm had established additional branches in Leeds and Glasgow along with its first expansion overseas with factories established in both South Africa and India.

Surprisingly during the depression years the firm continued to prosper - printing ink consumption actually increased by 10 per cent during those difficult years: Empire Trade Preference introduced in 1932 had given a boost to British manufactured goods and the packaging boom was starting. At the beginning of the decade Coates Brothers had around four per cent of the British market, far behind leaders such as Lorilleux & Bolton; Coates Brothers was perhaps tenth or eleventh in the league in 1930 but by 1940 had increased its market share to around eight per cent.

That growth was made possible by being the first ink company to take technology seriously; the first proper chemist was recruited in 1932 and by 1935 the Neoset two-phase drying principle was perfected - a

revolution in letterpress inks. Previously only rotary inks had dried entirely by absorption into the paper whereas all sheet fed letterpress inks were based on linseed oil and dried by oxidation; as a result of Coates research and development, high quality letterpress inks became touch dry in less than a minute instead of eight hours!

In 1937 the first formulation and production of Gravure and Flexo Inks were made at St Mary Cray. The following year the name CVP was first registered for resins and the same year the original Head Office site close to Fleet Street was moved to Easton Street at a cost of £50,000. (This was further developed in 1953 and another building purchased in 1953 followed by yet another building purchased in 1960 with access via an overhead walkway.)

Above: *A view of the black ink shop in 1936.* ***Top:*** *Staff gather for an annual outing in July 1925.*

Another important milestone was reached in 1939 when the first Heatset Inks were formulated and made at St Mary Cray.

There are several different kind of inks used for different kinds of printing: offset litho printing for example uses oxidation or ultra violet light for 'curing', gravure and flexo relies on evaporation of the solvent by heat, heatset web by a similar process of evaporation; cold-set relies on absorption whilst screen printing may rely on absorption, cure or heat. Each process requires a specific type of ink to ensure appropriate performance. Inks therefore have exact specifications for such characteristics as soap resistance or resistance to fading due to heat and light. Each colour has to be matched to the different pigment dispersions needed to meet customer requirement and to the specific paper, foil or plastic on which it is to be applied.

Having not only survived but prospered during the 1930s business collapsed in 1940 when the company was operating at a loss. Demand for printers' ink fell rapidly at the onset of war when paper became one of the first things to become in short supply. Things improved however when the firm was able to secure sub-contract work from the paint industry enabling the nucleus of the business to be kept intact.

Immediately after the war new branches or depots were opened in Birmingham and Dublin. The firm also began manufacturing metal coatings, an important addition to the firm's tin-printing inks. The future however was resins, a speciality developed as a result of paint contracts during the war years.

In 1948 a 45 acre site at Machen in South Wales was purchased and developed for CVP resins. The production of metal coating inks and litho plates were soon added to the product list.

A trip to Sydney in 1952 by 'Mr John' resulted in the first of a new wave of overseas investments when Coates acquired a small Australian ink company and secured a contract to supply Sun Gravure, a leading magazine printer in Australia.

In the following twenty years business continued to expand overseas with factories developed in Australia, New Zealand, Rhodesia, Singapore, Kenya, Hong Kong, Zambia, Trinidad, Jamaica, Nigeria and Ireland. That expansion was however concentrated in common-wealth and ex British Empire countries rather than in Europe or the USA.

Above: A company delivery van in 1932. Left: An aerial view of the St Mary Cray site pictured in 1947. Below: The same site in the early 1950s.

In 1968 a 13 acre ex-coal mine site was acquired at Midsomer Norton in Somerset. This was originally built to service a major liquid inks customer but gradually developed into the main manufacturing site for Gravure and Flexo inks. This was later to be developed into the main formulation and manufacturing site for Electro-static Toners and reprographic speciality products. That same year however also saw the first venture into Europe with the purchase of small ink companies in Denmark and Spain followed a year later by the company's first development in France when another small ink company was bought and moved to a new site.

In 1970 a site was purchased at Stallingborough for the further development of resin manufacture giving the company a presence in Manchester, Newcastle, Leeds, Glasgow, Birmingham, Belfast, Bristol and Dublin as well as Machen and St Mary Cray.

The mid 1970s saw further expansion and development of the St Mary Cray site plus the purchase of another building. This created the North Site for the original offset/web inks and the South Site was developed for screen and speciality products.

By 1977, the firm's centenary year, the firm employed more than 4,000 people, had three base factories in the UK and subsidiaries in more than 16 other countries.

Investment in France eventually led to a partnership with a French ink company called Lorilleux International which had roots going back to 1818 making it the world's oldest specialist ink producing company: it was then owned by CDF Chemie.

During the next two years there were changes in control with CDF Chemie changing its name to ORKEM; by mutual agreement in 1989 ORKEM increased its shareholding in Coates Lorilleux which later led to ownership by the Total Oil Group.

With the integration of Coates and Lorilleux business continued to expand in all market sectors within both European and overseas companies throughout the 1990s.

Above: *The engineering shop at St Mary Cray in 1951.* **Top:** *Factory staff pictured around 1950.* **Left:** *The 1951 edition of Drawdown, the house magazine produced by Coates Bros.*

The market segments and geographical spread appeared to create a perfect fit. However it still had relatively little business penetration into Germany and the USA although by the end of the decade it would do so.

During the 1990s Coates Lorilleux became part of the Total Petroleum Group of companies. In the first year of the new millennium however Coates Lorilleux had a new owner. Total decided to sell the ink business to the Sun Chemical company in order to focus on its own core business of oil and speciality chemicals.

The current high investment programme for Coates Lorilleux in the UK includes the St Mary Cray site which remains as head office for the UK business.

Coates Lorilleux is now an essential part of the Sun Chemical Group which is the largest company in its field in the world, with ink its core business.

Today Coates Lorilleux has an annual production of 140,000 tons of inks and has 5,000 employees world wide in over 40 countries. Turnover is in the region of £500 million each year; customers come from every sector of the printing industry: newspapers, magazines, journals, advertising, packaging and decoration.

At the beginning of the third millennium ink is a product subject to many demands: those dictated by rapid technical evolution of printing processes and those initiated in response to international legislation for the protection of the environment. There is a company commitment to control the selection of raw materials in terms of their safe use and potential problems with disposal. Coates Lorilleux applies the highest safety standards for all employees, customers and uses.

The world of ink manufacture is now a complex one, far removed from the simple inks of the 19th century when the Coates brothers established their small firm. They could not have foreseen the remarkable technical changes which would arrive during the 20th century nor guess how large the firm they founded would one day grow. Coates Lorilleux has come a long way since its modest origins. Some things we can be sure of: despite prophets of doom ringing the death knell of the printed word the day of the paperless office is a fantasy and the demand for printed products will never cease.

And as long as there is a demand for books and printed paper there will continue to be a demand for printers ink and the tradition which it encapsulates. It will come as no surprise to readers to know that Coates Lorilleux has provided its ink to the printers of this book to ensure that the traditions of quality established in 1877 continue to the present day.

Above left: Some of the printer supplies sold by Coates Bros in the 1950s. Top: Coates Bros in the early 1970s. Below: Production methods to satisfy today's modern market.

Wellers doing well

The Law: a word which can strike fear, apprehension and even terror in the hearts of many. Law has always been a complicated business. From Moses and the ten commandments, through the law tablets unearthed in Mesopotamia and onto the classical times of Greece and Rome, the law has always held a particular fascination and attraction for the best minds of each generation. In Roman times rhetoric and advocacy were essentials of a good education and members of the patrician classes were expected as a matter of course both to act as legal advocates and then serve as judges.

Whilst the knowledge and practice of Roman Law and the profession of lawyer may have faded in Britain during the Dark Ages, it was to reappear again centuries later under a different guise. Not least in the years following the Norman Conquest when English Law first appeared. English Law is based on local custom and practice rather than the codified continental system of law based on Roman principles and first began to be written down as legal precedent in the decades following the defeat of King Harold by William the Conqueror.

The writing down of local laws, the introduction of Statute law - laws imposed by the Sovereign, and later through Parliament, soon led to the re-emergence of a thriving legal profession. Or perhaps one should say legal professions with legal practitioners bearing a number of different names.

Today in England only two legal professions survive, distilled from their differing predecessors:

Above: An invoice from the mid 1930s.
Below: A view of the High Street in Bromley in the early 20th century. Wellers' offices at 162 High Street are above Medhursts.

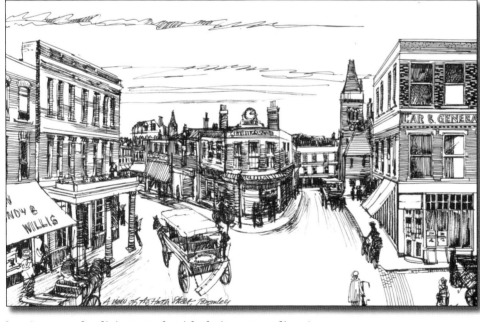

by themselves and briefing barristers to take on the more difficult or complex cases.

Today the barriers between these generalists and consultants are rapidly being eroded with solicitors increasingly specialising and handling far more of the work traditionally done by barristers - nothing remains static, not even in something as traditionally conservative as the legal profession.

barristers and solicitors each with their own traditions and skills.

Barristers became professional advocates, specialising in particular aspects of the law and using their skills in the higher courts; solicitors by contrast became the general practitioners of law handling routine matters

Above: An artist's impression of High Street, Bromley in the days before motorised vehicles.
Top: A school photo taken in 1920s, Mr Lloyd can be seen fifth from the right on the second row down.

It is a sad fact of life that people only consult a solicitor when they see no other alternative. Too expensive, too long winded, too inflexible are but a few of the reasons given. But it is often the case that sound advice at the outset can save time and money in the long run. And one firm that knows something of the long run is the Bromley legal firm of Wellers solicitors.

A tradition of legal excellence and service began in 1881 when George Weller first started practising as a solicitor at premises at 35 Victoria Street, London EC.

The Law Society

By Authority of the Council, We do hereby Certify

that Mr *Cecil Evan Tenison Lloyd* having been duly elected, is appointed and admitted a **Member** of **The Law Society**. Dated this *17th* day of *January* One thousand nine hundred and *Forty-four*.

Secretary.

President.

Working at that time on his own, he had offices in numerous locations. His first recorded period of work in Bromley was in 1883.

While being based at that office, he also practised in other towns in the area over the next few years, including Deptford, Greenwich, Sevenoaks and Maidstone. It was, however, his son WG Weller (or 'WG' as he was affectionately known) who made both a lasting impression on those who knew him and a significant contribution to the high local reputation of the firm.

He was a forceful advocate, and his reputation extended far beyond the boundaries of his home county, Kent. He was admitted to the Register of the Law Society in 1904 and was very much in the stern Edwardian mould of a solicitor, with a renowned sharpness of mind that instilled fear into many a solicitor or barrister who encountered him. A well-known Court of Appeal Judge recalled his own early years as a barrister when he confronted the 'formidable old WG' in the local court. His Honour Judge Sir Gerald Hurst QC, on taking his seat at the reopening of Bromley County Court after the summer vacation following WG's death in 1951; paid tribute to him,

Top: The certificate given to Mr Cecil Lloyd upon his admission into the Law Society in 1944.
Above right: Wellers' premises at 39 Chatterton Road, which they occupied until January 1991.

saying, 'I feel that we should not let the opportunity pass of expressing this Court's appreciation of the work of Mr Weller over many years. He was for long a great friend of ours and we all owe a debt of gratitude to him for his work as an advocate, in which he was an untiring pursuer of the course of true justice. He was all that an advocate should be'. Mr TA Grose from WH

A member of Bromley Rotary Club who followed in WG's footsteps as president recalled an occasion before World War II when they had a speaker who began to expound Nazi propaganda. Mr Weller courageously stood up and said they should hear this man no more. The club promptly backed him up and the speaker was requested to leave.

Mr HW Bird, senior Bromley Probation Officer, was impressed with WG's thoroughness, conscientiousness and integrity. Others knew him as a man of wide knowledge and cultivated intellect.

House and Sons, Solicitors, Sevenoaks speaking on behalf of solicitors practising at the court said that his firm's association with Mr Weller had extended over 40 years and for many years a strong friendship existed between them.

'Mr Weller had been an example to the profession for many years'. Mr Geoffrey Lovegrove, barrister, said that not only on behalf of members of the Bar appearing at Bromley, but for the Bar in general, to whom Mr Weller was so well known, he wished to express appreciation of his friendship and to testify to the great affection in which he was held by them all.

WG Weller made a great and lasting contribution to the local community. He was for some years a Town Councillor and from 1907 to 1951 (the year of his death) he served on Bromley Library Committee, where his 'terrific' knowledge of books was of the greatest assistance. Throughout his life he retained the deepest interest in the activities and progress of the Borough of Bromley.

He was the founder-president of the Bromley Rotary Club where he was known as a hard-working, unsentimental man of the highest integrity who gave great service to the community at large and to particular individuals. Apart from holding the office of president, WG had 28 years active service in the club, which was thought to have been a record at the time.

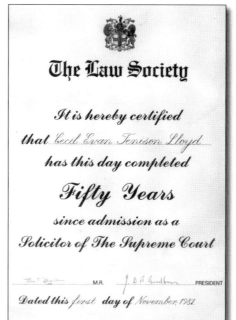

Upon WG's death the firm passed into the ownership of his nephew, Mr R Duncan Birrell, when the firm became known as Weller and Birrell, of 162 High Street, Bromley, above what is now Allders. After Mr Birrell ceased to practise as a solicitor in 1957 Cecil Lloyd took over the practice. He was joined by ESA 'Ted' Hubbard and together they established a Christian element in the practice which has lasted ever since. Three years later the two went into partnership and the name of the firm was changed to Wellers. Ted Hubbard is still connected with the firm, is well-known as Elder Statesman in the town and sat for many years as a Deputy District Judge in local County Courts. Indeed the practice has produced no less than four District Judges over recent years.

The firm has had a long-standing association with Bromley Football Club and on the occasion of the Club's Centenary, offered its congratulations by donating the Wellers' Centenary Cup to the Club. The fortunes of the footballers are followed with great interest by the firm.

Above: The certificate awarded to Mr Lloyd in 1987 to commemorate his 50 years as a solicitor.
Top: Wellers partners pictured in 1984 (from left to right) Michael Lee, Tony Summers, David Lamdin, Paul Martin, Stephen Scott and Ted Hubbard (seated).

Over the years the practice has expanded and has had offices in Sevenoaks, Chatterton Road, the High Street and Lownds Avenue as well as presently at Tweedy Road and more recently, in London.

The Lownds Avenue site was needed by the Council for redevelopment of Bromley town centre and the firm moved all its business to its Tweedy Road offices. Accommodation at this site was extended in 1988 to provide a base for the company's growing commercial department and renamed Tenison House as a permanent memorial to Cecil Evan Tenison Lloyd, who retired as senior partner in

Above: The firm's office at 2 Lownds Avenue, Bromley, now replaced by the Glades Shopping Centre. Right: The foundations of the Tenison House extension beginning to take shape in 1987.
Below: Roger Sims, MP (right) pictured opening the extension in 1988, with Cecil Lloyd in the wheelchair.

1978; the new office was opened by Chislehurst MP Roger Sims. Sadly Cecil Lloyd died a year after the opening of the new extension. The scope of Wellers' expertise is considerable ranging from family matters and personal affairs, to company/commercial law, litigation, property (both residential and commercial), charitable trusts and employment law among other areas. Tony Summers is a member of the Law Society's Personal Injury Panel and the firm is in association with law firms in the USA as well as the Middle and Far East. The firm also has a growing London office in Lincoln's Inn Fields, an asset when it comes to providing central London facilities for its developing number of national and international corporate clients. An important development in recent times has been the co-operation of Wellers with the Veco Trust (UK) Ltd. Together the companies can offer businesses a complete cost-effective professional service for legal, accounting, tax and other company administration matters. This comes at a time when the business community is faced with ever more complex procedures stemming from the global market-place for goods and personnel. In addition the firm has launched a legal audit programme, 'Lawplus', exclusively available from Wellers. This service is

designed to help businesses keep their heads above water in the flood of current business legislation from the UK and Europe.

The company has always had a strong family base and gains much of its business through personal recommendation. In line with its history of good practice it has developed specialised departments and has recently produced its own quality manual; this was a contributing factor to the firm achieving the recognition of the quality award ISO 9001 in the early part of 2000. Expressed in its quality statement is a commitment on the part of both Partners and staff involved with clients 'to seek to provide the widest possible range of legal services tailored to each individual client's needs'. To achieve this each department is required to monitor the level of its performance and submit to an annual review. In this way the Partners at Wellers seek to maintain the standards set by their illustrious predecessor.

In spite of its growing commercial client base Wellers is still very much a family firm and has provided legal advice and assistance to many families throughout the generations - work which includes preparation of wills, the administration of estates and trusts as well as, sadly, divorce, separation and child custody matters.

Financial services are an ever growing minefield. Wellers can procure specialist advice in tax and investment matters from the stock market, tax counsel and investment advisers; all within the protection of the Financial Services Act. Wellers' litigation department by contrast aims to help those involved in disputes.

The firm's first advice to clients is however to make every effort to resolve matters before resorting to the courts. In fact early involvement of Wellers' services could save expensive court costs and legal fees with good independent professional advice. Wellers has been giving such advice now for well over a century and can assist in all aspects of Landlord and Tenant law. Commercial property too is a field of expertise for the firm. To buy or to lease? Wellers has demonstrated a high level of skill and awareness in the buying and selling of businesses, leases and property development. On a similar topic Wellers will oversee a company's transactions with the emphasis on prevention rather than cure. Good legal

advice at the start of a business venture will help prevent difficulties arising later.

Risks are of course part of running a business. Businessmen and women weigh up the facts then make an informed decision. But one area where no business should take a risk is with the law. The law is a potential minefield for businesses: there are currently more than 200 offences for example for which a company director can be held personally liable under UK legislation and directors are increasingly liable for their company's actions. This can frequently apply to situations such as wrongful trading, health and safety, environmental issues, breach of Companies Act requirements and failure to exercise reasonable care and skill when carrying out duties. Busy directors cannot keep up with current legislation, but fortunately they do not need to: Wellers and its 'Lawplus' scheme offers a tailor-made legal service to meet exactly this kind of problem.

Wellers' offices now dominate a corner of an increasingly developing part of the town of Bromley, symbolic of the firm's commitment to be in the thick of activity whether commercial, litigious or involving the complexities of everyday domestic or working life.

Professional legal services, guiding the public through the mysteries of the law is an honourable profession with roots extending back thousands of years - that proud tradition is surely nowhere more honoured than at the Bromley firm of Wellers Solicitors, building on the traditions of the past while embracing the 21st century world of e.commerce and the internet revolution.

Below: *The partners in the year 2000, (left to right) Paul Martin, Tony Summers, Stephen Scott and Alistair Crow.*

Memories of Churchill

Bromley is the home of a great British success story - Churchill Insurance. Not only has Churchill seen amazing growth and increasing market share in its first decade of trading, by producing products and service which are appreciated by its customers, it has also made the selling and follow-up of insurance policies fun for its staff - no small achievement. Churchill Insurance was founded by chairman and chief executive Martin Long, whose experience with UK insurers convinced him that British customers deserved a far better service from their insurers.

The market for motor insurance in the UK was transformed in the 1980s, because of changing customer needs and expectations. A huge growth in car ownership brought massively increased demand, since more people were driving more cars more often, and there were therefore more accidents. In addition increasing sophistication of car design tended to increase repair costs. At the same time, household budgets were under pressure and customers were looking for lower insurance costs.

> *The company began life on 19 June 1989 with 88 employees*

Martin Long approached Swiss giant Winterthur, (now part of the Credit Suisse Group - one of the top ten financial organisations in the world) to fund a new company. This confidence in both Winterthur and the British public proved to be well founded and Churchill embarked on an amazing period of growth. The name of the company embodies many of its attributes: Britishness, trust, strength, and success. The company began life on 19 June 1989 with 88 employees (25 of which are still with the company ten years later) selling car insurance policies, and added home products the following year. Today, Churchill has 1.8 million customers and over 2,700 employees in the UK 1,500 of them in Bromley.

The company's success is based on giving its customers exceptional service. It is the vision of the company to deliver the unquestioned, publicly acknowledged best customer service in the insurance industry in the world. In addition it prides itself on providing a progressive and exciting

Below: *Churchill's first suite of offices in Starts Hill Avenue, Farnborough.*

The team spirit and sense of togetherness at Churchill is unusual and unique. The company expects hard work and commitment from its people; but is also highly supportive. Staff find it fun and rewarding to work towards the long service awards at three, five and ten years. The company offers many benefits including a non-contributory pension scheme, medical support and staff discounts on its insurance products. 'Top Dogs' and 'Star Performer' status are awarded for extraordinary contributions to the company and a Hall of Fame recognises truly

work environment and offering its staff training and development programmes which provide plenty of opportunities for promotion. The company is characterised by a flat and remarkably open structure. The ethos of the company is one of continuous improvement, and everyone is encouraged to make suggestions - in 1999 alone the staff made 2,548 suggestions.

Top: *Churchill House - the company's first flagship office premises.*
Above: *'Windy City' - the old Westmoreland Place which Churchill completely re-built.*

exceptional performance (all carrying significant rewards). Employees are actually exhorted to have fun and enjoy their work. This commitment to caring for their staff has been directly recognised by the company being granted the Investors in People Award, a national standard for best practice in training and developing employees and by their earning a place in the book 'Britain's Top Employers' - the best 100 companies to work for in Britain. In 1998 it received a Human Resources Excellence Award in 'Employee Development'. A pilot scheme recently introduced for Modern Apprenticeships was one of the first UK programmes to provide fast track NVQ

accreditation course and a number of company employees have already benefited from it.

Other accolades received by the company include the coveted ISO 9002 accreditation (the only internationally recognised quality award for service companies) and the Plain English Crystal Mark of approval for their insurance policy booklets. Churchill was voted Best Car and Home Insurance Provider by the Guardian and Observer newspapers in their Consumer Finance Awards in March 2000 - the first award of its kind. On

that occasion, Martin Long expressed his delight at winning such a prestigious award, which was based on the results of 4,500 questionnaires: ìThe award was based on such issues as friendliness of staff, quality of literature and flexibility of policy. I am particularly pleased that the quality of our service is continually recognised - on this occasion by

customers, the most important people.î It achieved the Best Internet Provider for Home Insurance, Best Internet Provider for Motor Insurance and Best Direct Motor Insurance Provider in the Your Money Direct Awards in May 2000. A Mori poll taken in April 2000 found that 83 per cent of the population recognise Churchill as a leading brand.

Churchill staff are completely free to do whatever they like to delight customers and they do. Since February 1997, the company has enjoyed a further radical initiative: Say Yes Not No (SYNN). Staff are not allowed to say no to a customer without permission - very different from most companies, especially insurers.

Top: *Churchill Court - Churchill's prestigious headquarters at Bromley South.*
Above: *Churchill at play - celebrating their success at their anniversary ball.*

It is the responsibility of every person who works at Churchill to make their customers feel unique, special and the object if their attention. Customers are constantly being asked to comment on the service. Over 300,000 did so in 1999 and of those making a claim in that year over 98 per cent said they would recommend the company to their family and friends. Such figures speak for themselves.

Churchill has an impressive record of innovation. Their 'firsts' include service guarantees; wholly-owned garages to ensure the highest standards of repairs (with the first being opened in 1995); courtesy cars for customers when their own is off the road; a customer loyalty programme and a unique fire prevention system for thatched

Below: Work hard and play hard - fancy dress days play their part in making Churchill such a unique and fun place to work.

properties - plus many other things. Always ahead of the competition, Churchill established an Internet site in 1995.

In a typical move, the company opened an IT software subsidiary in India in 1996, linked to Britain by satellite. This supports Churchill's software which brought it a source of excellent, well-educated programmers; and allowed it to process development work round the clock - a great competitive and cost reducing advantage.

In 1994, Churchill presented its unique symbol to the world, the bulldog, which personifies its business spirit of solid reliability and strength. When a new TV commercial was launched in 1996, the dog proved an instant hit. So much so that following hundreds of requests Churchill had to start producing replicas. In July 1997 the first Churchill nodding dogs went on sale and 1,000 were sold during the first week alone.

This has proved to be an enduringly popular symbol for the company and is held in great affection by many people throughout the country.

The company's business strategy of increasing growth not only organically but also through acquisitions and business partnerships has been tremendously successful. In 1995 they acquired a major portfolio of household customers from Refuge Assurance. Over the next few years Churchill acquired Anglia Countrywide, Devitt Insurance Services and the National Insurance & Guarantee Corporation Plc (NIG).

In 1996, they formed a partnership with Halifax (at the time the UK's largest building society) which became the first of many partnerships leading to Churchill's recognition as the industry's No 1 outsourcer. Other partnerships include branded car insurance for Lloyds TSB and home insurance for the Co-operative Bank.

Through all these various activities, Churchill is now present in all the major distribution channels of their industry.

Due to rapid growth and continually increasing business levels Churchill expanded into Teesside in January 1999 with the opening of a second call centre and thus created 300 new jobs in the area.

However, the company has always been based in the London Borough of Bromley. From the very first humble beginnings in a small suite of offices in Starts Hill Avenue, they opened their first central Bromley offices in January 1989 in a four-storey office building in London Road named Churchill House. By 1993 the company's extraordinary success meant that staff numbers had grown significantly. They therefore overflowed into the nearby Bank of America tower block and also took possession of a large unit on an industrial estate in Biggin Hill where all the

Top: *Churchill are very active in raising money for charity. As an example, in the last 10 years they have raised over £110,000 for the Foundation for Children with Leukaemia. This picture shows Martin Long presenting Ray Allen and Graham Cole with their most recent cheque.*
Above: *The nationally famous Churchill dog.*

document processing and filing work takes place to this day.

The phenomenal growth continued and so Churchill leased further office space in Hanover Place, an award winning refurbishment of a 1950s cinema in Ravensbourne Road. For a time the company was therefore located in four different buildings, a necessary but not very desirable short-term solution to the 'problems' created by success.

However, it was always a long-term objective of the company to have all the Bromley based operations under one roof.

In November 1994, after many months of negotiations with the existing owners and town planners, Churchill purchased Westmoreland Place - the very dated 1960s concrete shopping/office complex and tower at Bromley South known locally as 'windy city'. Very early on it was agreed that to refurbish the whole building was imprac-tical due to its limiting structural design. Where possible, Churchill retained and adapted parts of the old structure so that the final building is now mainly re-built but also partly re-furbished.

The building was constructed in three consecutive phases to coincide with the lease expiry dates on the other premises and step by step, Churchill Court was built. The third and final phase was completed and celebrated with a traditional topping-out ceremony in June 1999. Perfect timing as Churchill were celebrating their tenth anniversary at the same time.

A long-standing aim had been achieved - all 1,500 Bromley based members of staff had a new home under one roof in a landmark, award-winning building. A building of which Churchill and the people of Bromley can be proud. It was completed on time and on budget.

Above: *Martin Long, the Founder of Churchill Insurance.*

And now Churchill is racing into the future. One of the many exciting challenges is the planned expansion of the Internet side of the business. Much development has already taken place in this field since Churchill went live on the Internet in August 1995. In October 1999 an interactive website for both car and home insurance quota-tions and sales was launched. This has proved popular in spite of the fact that it has not, as yet, been very actively promoted. In addition, Churchill believes that e-commerce offers enormous opportunities for after-sales service and a range of new web-based services is planned which will allow customers to amend their cover, report new claims and generally check on the up to date position of their insurance arrangements.

Martin Long recently summed up the challenges facing Churchill in the years ahead, 'Quality of customer service repre-sents the only long-term competitive advantage. Products, IT and strategy can all be copied, but outstanding customer service cannot be replicated overnight. We have worked hard since 1989 to delight every single customer'. Churchill will continue to provide their award winning, unrivalled, world class service. They will continue their complete focus on people - staff and customers. Their clear strategy will continue to be implemented by great staff who keep their customers happy and thereby create value.

In the Corporate Research Foundation's publication Britain's Top Employers (mentioned earlier), they offer the summary 'Although Churchill's market place will continue to remain highly competitive, the company has a genuine edge based on a radical vision, a deep commitment to customer care and staff devel-opment, and a refreshingly different way of operating. All these attributes made Churchill truly one of Britain's top employers'.

All of Churchill's qualities serve to ensure that Churchill Insurance has a bright future, continuing as an enormous contributor to the wealth of the local economy and offering outstanding career opportunities to the people of Bromley.

Both pages: The old Central Library on High street is shown to good effect in these two shots of the 1960s. In common with most public buildings erected in the early years of the twentieth century, the Library managed to combine some graceful architectural features with an air of solidity and durability. However pleasing to the eye, however, the Library was still a place of work as the first photograph shows *(above)*. In March 1966 Bromley Central Library was playing its part in contributing books to the National Library Week Exhibition. The wagon was awaiting its load, and no doubt plenty of strenuous work lay ahead in the task of filling it. The organisation of the operation was in the hands of the Borough Librarian, Mr AH Watkins, who is pictured in the foreground along with Mr RG Surridge and another colleague. The year 1966 was an important one in the history of the Library in that it marked the Diamond Jubilee of its opening in 1906. The well-known philanthropist, Andrew Carnegie, had offered £7,500 for the purpose of building a new public library in Bromley,

and an ideal site on the High Street had presented itself in the shape of 'Neelgherries'. This was the name of Miss Emily Dowling's house, which had been bequeathed by her to the people of Bromley at her death in 1900. Hence the contents of the existing public library, which formed part of the School of Science and Art Building in Tweedy Road, were transferred to the fine new edifice erected on the site of 'Neelgherries'. If the new Library looked as if it might last forever, this was not to be the case, and the demolition contractor's sign on the second photograph *(left)* tells its own sad story. By this date, July 1969, the Library was empty, closed and awaiting its end, for the decision had been made to construct a grand new library and theatre complex. Yet again Mr Watkins had found himself in charge of a book moving operation - this time on a massive scale. Around 150,000 books were transferred to temporary accommodation in 1968, this being the old School of Science and Art building in Tweedy Road. It might be said that, for the time being, the Library had gone 'back to its roots!'

Wellcome research at Langley Court

One of the world's best known company's is the pharmaceuticals giant Glaxo Wellcome. The company's local associations go back many years and few natives of the Bromley area can be unaware of the firm's large estate at Langley Court in Beckenham's South Eden Park Road.

It was in 1919, shortly after the end of the first world war, that the millionaire and philanthropist Henry Wellcome bought what was then a 105 acre site at Langley Court for £32,000. Wellcome conveyed the estate to his Wellcome Foundation in 1924.

The existence of what is now the Langley Court Estate can be traced from very early times. Some have even suggested that the earliest known reference to the land which later became the Langley Estate is an Anglo-Saxon charter dated 862 AD now in the British Museum. The truth or otherwise however is lost in the mists of antiquity.

The land did however form part of the vast portion of Kent which was assigned to Odo Bishop of Bayeux by William the Conqueror. The Langley name became directly associated with the land which is now known as Langley Park from 1350 when the Langley family first owned the estate.

For the following five centuries the present Glaxo Wellcome Langley Court Estate was part of that much larger Langley Estate, and within that domain being a mere portion of the area long known as Langley Farm.

Until his death on 29th June 1820 both the Langley and adjacent Kelsey Estates were owned by the first Lord Gwydyr who had inherited the Langley Estate from his grandmother Amy Burrell who had died in 1789. The Estate was inherited by Peter Burrell III (son of Lord Gwydyr and the first baronet of that name).

The second Lord Gwydyr, who by then had also become Lord Willoughby de Eresby, did not need the Langley and Kelsey Estates and they were accordingly broken up in a great sale which took place on 31st October 1820. At that auction sale, which took place at the Garraways Coffee House Change Alley, Cornhill, the Langley domains were offered by auctioneers Skinner, Tuchin and Forest in three separate lots: Langley Park, Langley Farm and Langley Lodge.

Those estates offered for sale by the second Lord Gwydyr were extensive comprising 3,202 acres in and around Beckenham, Bromley, West Wickham, Hayes, Keston, Lewisham and Sydenham.

Top: *An aerial view of Langley Court in the days of the Bucknall family.* ***Above right:*** *Croquet on the lawn in 1902.* ***Right:*** *Staff playing croquet in 1944.* ***Below:*** *A member of the Bucknall family outside the Coach House, 1900.*

At the auction the three Langley plots were purchased by one Emmanuel Goodheart.

Under Emmanuel Goodheart the Langley properties were well maintained. Several pictures of the mansion and gardens from those times still exist in the local history section of the Bromley Central Library.

One interesting architectural feature of the Mansion is that the Star of David appears on all the cast iron rainwater hoppers. The Langley farmhouse had been demolished to make way for the Mansion but some of the original kitchen

gardens were retained in beds around the house; the idea is said to have been that rainwater passing through the hoppers was then blessed on its way to the plants.

On the death of his father in 1853 Charles Emmanuel Goodheart inherited the Langley properties. In 1884 however CE Goodheart decided to sell the mansion and part of Langley Farm to JL Bucknall, a sale which was completed on 13th November 1884.

The Bucknall family was in shipping and cruised the world and had an especial affinity for the Far East and Japan. On his trips JL Bucknall would collect unusual plants most of which were planted in the North Field and around the North Lodge. As a result an architect was inspired to design the local garage in a pagoda style, distinctly Japanese architecture and 'not Chinese'. But that didn't stop locals referring to it as the Chinese garage and the name stuck. When the car sales franchise was separated from the Texaco petrol station the company took on the Chinese Garage name.

The Bucknall family continued to live at Langley Court until around 1914 at which stage they ran into financial difficulties. According to folklore the family were amongst those who had underwritten the insurance for the Titanic, and when it sank they sank too.

Langley Court and its estate was thereafter left unoccupied for a time and during the 1914-18 war it as used as a camp for officer prisoners of war.

Above left: *The stables in 1964.*
Left: *Building 79 CRL, 1947.*
Below: *Members of the Packing and Filling department, Building 5, 1956.*

Following Henry Wellcome's acquisition of the estate a limited number of new buildings were erected mainly to accommodate the research work and production of vaccines and serological products.

For some years the 'Bucknall' mansion was utilised as laboratories and administration offices. During the second world war, 1939-45, a block of chemical research laboratories was built as well as extensive facilities for the production of penicillin by the bottle process. This process

In 1918 when Henry S Wellcome wished to move what was then the Wellcome Physiological Research Laboratories from its home at Brockwell Park he was able to acquire the run down Langley Court estate at a very favourable price. The purchase included the present mansion and other buildings together with 105 acres of land.

Henry Wellcome bought the property from AL Bucknall on 16th October 1919 through his agent H Griffiths.

Possibly Henry Wellcome did not wish to assign the Langley Court property to any single Burroughs Wellcome company and so he awaited the consolidation of his world-wide commercial interests into a new organisation called the Wellcome Foundation Ltd which he created in 1924. Once that consolidation had been achieved the conveyance of the Langley Court property to the Wellcome Foundation Ltd followed on 17th July 1924.

was made obsolete by the deep fermentation method which, although not adopted for penicillin, was later extensively developed for the manufacture of Interferon.

The facilities were converted after the war into biochemical laboratories. After 1945 and particularly from around 1950 onwards the Wellcome Foundation expanded its activities tremendously, particularly in the chemotherapeutic field. In addition great advances were made in the vaccines such as polio vaccine, veterinary vaccines and many other similar products. Those major developments necessitated the building of many new laboratories on the Langley Court Estate including those for Pharmacology, Tropical Medicine, Physical Chemistry and a variety of buildings concerned with the production of biological products.

At the same time the clinical research side of the company's a activities was greatly expanded. That also required the construction of substantial purpose designed buildings.

During the 1980s extensive redevelopment of the site took place creating an architectural mix sympathetic

Top: Pharmacology in the Mansion, 1957, Dave Tulett, left and Fred Huggins, right.
Above: Innoculating Thomson Flasks for Diptheria, 1948.
Right: An aerial view of the site in 1966.

with the Kentish traditions of the rural parklands of Langley Court.

A number of new facilities particularly for Clinical Research, Pharmacology, Drug Safety Evaluation, Information Science and Project Management were established and whilst those developments took place ecological

developments were also implemented: a lake and hillside were created with 500 trees planted and 30,000 shrubs.

From the Wellcome point of view it was fortunate that CE Goodheart sold part of the Langley Farm Estate to JL Bucknall in 1884. If that sale had not taken place the Langley Court Estate now owned by Glaxo Wellcome would probably have been built over as was much of rest of the former Langley lands. The urban development of the area surrounding Langley Court has however been carefully planned and the site is now surrounded by high-class residential property, schools and recreation grounds.

By the mid 1990s the Langley Court estate consisted of 107 acres of land containing 12 acres of buildings, 15 acres of roads and 9 acres of car parks. The site contained 136 buildings containing approximately 5,000 rooms.

The estate passed into the ownership of Glaxo Wellcome in 1995 as part of a merger between the two companies. Soon after, some of the land was sold for commercial use and some for residiential developemnt as the size of the site decreased and staff were relocated to other Group facilities. Nevertheless, the heritage continues today and Beckenham is still playing an important role in the research, development and manufacturing of medicines for serious diseases.

Above left: *Chemists pictured in 1971.*
Left: *An aerial picture taken in 1994.*
Below: *A recent staff gathering.*

Seventy five years of excellence in printing

The company was founded in 1925 by Arthur George Bishop and initially was based near Billingsgate fish market at 9 Lovat Lane in the City of London, before expanding across the street to encompass number 28. Jobs often had to be carried across the narrow cobbled street between the two buildings. This presented a number of hazards. Not only did the jobs have to be covered with a wrapper to protect them from the weather, but it was not unknown for live eels to escape from the fish porters' boxes, which they carried on their heads, onto the cobbles as they were being carried to and from the market, causing hazards under foot. Other forms of wildlife were discouraged by the regular visits of the rat catcher and his dog.

Initially the company concentrated on the production of stationery, particularly envelopes, before moving into letterpress printing. In the early days much of the work was highly labour intensive with typesetting in metal, or wood, by hand. Printing was done on small handfed letterpress machines. In the mid-1930s A G Bishop was joined in the company by his sons Arthur and Gordon, after they had served their apprenticeships at the Lewes Press in Sussex.

The second world war brought difficult times for the company. Both sons volunteered for active service as did many of the staff. Luckily the staff and the buildings survived the war intact, but further difficulties arose with paper rationing after the war. All of this contributed to considerable uncertainty and disruption. However, the company quickly began to recover and on the return of the two sons from the war, the business was incorporated as a limited company.

Above: Company founder Arthur George Bishop.
Right: *A drawing by Pearl West of Bishop's premises in Lovat Lane.*

By 1955 the company had outgrown its premises at Lovat Lane and the decision was made to move. The present site was bought at St Mary Cray for £10,000 and 5,000 square feet of factory and offices were erected at a cost of some £29,000. The factory was extended in the 1960s to the present size of 10,000 square feet.

Since the 1960s there have been rapid and fundamental changes in printing technology. In 1960 the company installed its first small litho printing machine, which could only print one colour at a time. This is in contrast to the present machines which can print up to five colours at once on a much larger sheet.

Film typesetting was introduced in 1980, only to be replaced in 1988 by Apple Macintosh digital typesetting. Technology has again moved on so that now all scanning of pictures, page make-up and imposition is done electronically. The increasing use of computers means that in the future printers will have to offer a total communications service, including marketing, design, data handling and mailing.

The present managing director, Christopher, grandson of A G Bishop, was trained in printing technology and management at the London School (now College) of Printing. While still a student he won the Howard Hazell Scholarship and two years later in 1958 won the Gold Medal for graphic design awarded by the British Federation of Master Printers (now the British Printing Industries Federation). This was recognised by Prime Minister Harold Macmillan who sent a personal letter of congratulation.

The part of the business which has remained unchanged is its commitment to the highest levels of quality and service. This is reflected in the company's mission statement of 'Modern methods combined with old-fashioned values'.

In order to keep pace with a changing market Bishops has constantly invested in updating its equipment, undergoing a major expansion programme in 1994 which dramatically changed its working methods. The majority of Bishops work is now brochures, reports, books and business stationery, where colour is ever more evident.

Above: Christopher Bishop receiving his Gold Medal from Lord McCorquodale, on behalf of the British Federation of Master Printers, in 1958. **Right:** The three original Bishops outside St Mary Cray offices in 1970. **Below:** A view of the machine room in the early 1960s.

Heather Dunsdon, the company's customer services manager is currently working towards a BA in Print Management and Technology, and in 1999 was Student of the Year at the London College of Printing.

Bishops is still a family business with several of the staff having been with the company for over 20 years; notably Dave Dennison, printing department manager who joined the company as an apprentice over 40 years ago. In fact, romance blossomed when he met and married Wendy who was working in the binding department at the time.

In 1989 Christopher Bishop organised a buy back of equity to keep the company within the immediate family, and his wife Betty is company secretary. He is currently a director of the recently formed Bromley Enterprise Partnership Ltd and in 1992 was elected a Freeman of the City of London, an honour which he feels reflects the involvement of the company and his ancestors in the city over many years.

The company has continued to encourage staff training. Production director Terry Thornhill was awarded the Sir Henry Fildes Prize by the Institute of Management as the best student nationally in 1998 after gaining an NVQ level 5 Diploma in Management. He is currently studying for an MBA with the Open University.

Top left: Jack Congrave with his wife Jean upon his retirement in June 1998. Jack had worked for the company for 24 years, initially as Works Manager, then as Works Director.
Top right: Two teams entered for a local fun sports day in 1991.
Above: Heather Dunsdon (Customer Services Manager), Terry Thornhill (Production Director) and Sue Swann (Reception). *Above left:* An aerial view of the premises at St Mary Cray.
Right: Christopher Bishop with Dave Dennison, machine room overseer. The firm's longest ever serving member of production staff.

Helping to improve Bromley's homes

Frank Donald Voyce, known as Don to his friends, was a cabinet maker by trade before he started his own business in 1945. He began in Bromley high street with a workshop repairing bomb damaged furniture, whilst his daughter-in-law, Olive, did the books. A year later the company became FD Voyce and Son Ltd. on the return of Frank's son Eric from wartime service with the Navy. The business expanded quickly and in 1947 and 1948 a shop was let in Widmore Road to sell second hand furniture.

Whilst Olive was expecting their second child, she and Eric decided to lease a flat and shop at 32 East Street for the princely sum of £3 per week. Eric was unsure exactly what to do with the shop and decided to consult his father who suggested a hobby shop. This seemed like a good idea as they had been very popular before the war. Setting up the shop took a lot of hard work and some imagination. The premises had previously been a fish shop and all the old fish slabs had to be cleared out. The next problem was the relative lack of start up capital, only £100. This bought relatively little stock which had to be carefully spread out around the walls. The business quickly flourished into what was to become one of the first do-it-yourself shops, reflecting the growing public interest in home improvements in the post war years. As the do-it-yourself business prospered in the 1950s the decision was taken to close down the second hand furniture shops. This enabled the family business to buy the shops on either side of their premises on East Street, numbers 30 and 34, previously a butchers and a florists. The extra room this gave the family allowed them to extend their product lines into a wood yard and Liden Whitewood furniture. The family later bought the freehold on all three shops.

The business had a lucky escape during a fire in 1968. The fire broke out in an asbestos woodstore in the yard at the back of the shop.

Above: Frank Donald Voyce pictured in the shop in 1960. *Below:* The DIY shop pictured in 1948.

The local newspaper records that it took four fire tenders to control the flames, holding up busy shopping day traffic in the process. Luckily the firemen managed to confine the flames to the storehouse and the only damage was to stock and sawing machinery.

In the early 1970s the company, now trading under the name of Voyce of Bromley, leased number 10 East Street. This site was used as a kitchen, bathroom and bedroom showroom, reflecting the public's growing interest in fitted furniture, especially kitchens. The Voyce family also began to offer a design and fitting service.

Their first suppliers were Hygena and Grovewood who were making the move away from flatpack units into individually designed fitted kitchens, the cost of which would have been around £1, 500. Although this was a lot of money at the time it is nothing compared to the amounts that people are prepared to invest today in order to achieve the perfect 'look' for their home, and hopefully add some value to it!

Above: *Voyce's first fitted kitchen showroom.*
Top: *The shop in the early 1970s.*

As people were increasingly prepared to spend more and more money on their homes the family decided to expand their do-it-yourself shop. In 1972 they bought number 36 East Street, which had previously been Bargain Wallpaper and was later to become Fads. Whilst the site was being redeveloped the family's do-it-yourself store temporarily moved to West Street. The new showroom opened in 1973, the basement became the DIY store and the ground floor became a kitchen showroom. The top three floors of the building were leased to other companies as offices. In 1972 a water store was introduced selling water softeners and treatment units which has proved a highly successful addition to the family's business.

In 1998 the company closed the do-it -yourself department and the basement of the building is now leased to a local nightclub. This allowed them to concentrate on the kitchen side of the business which has continued to go from strength to strength. Today the family concentrate on medium and top range quality kitchens. They design individual kitchens for individual clients to create anything from a traditional farmhouse look to the latest in European chic, or minimalist style. The company's team of experienced staff do everything from measuring the client's kitchen to supervising installation, with the dedicated design team scouring Europe to provide the very best range of styles. The company has now moved into the future, and e-commerce, with the launch of their website in 2000. This move is a reflection of the family's talent for spotting emerging trends and adapting their business to capitalise upon them.

However it is also a move based upon sound business sense. The company provides kitchens for clients from London to the coast. Voyce's see the extension of their business further afield as a potential area for growth and the website will allow them to reach the wider

design side of the business. He has recently been followed into the company by his daughter Hannah, who now helps to design the kitchens after having completed a design degree at university. Ken's wife, Sheila does the accounts and one of the most recent additions to the staff is Marion's son Daniel who is carrying on the family tradition of working for the company during his school holidays. Staff loyalty is strong as proved by Phil Blackwell who has worked alongside Andy in the kitchen planning department for over 22 years.

range of customers they will need for this expansion. However the company still remains very much a family business. All of Eric and Olive Voyce's five children have worked in the shops on Saturdays and some of them have worked for the company full time. This includes Robert Voyce who worked his way up from delivery boy to Managing Director and played an integral part in the development of the fitted kitchen business in the early 1970s; Ken Voyce who now runs the Water Store; Marion Hooson, the youngest daughter, is also a director who runs the front desk. In 1972 Eric and Olive's son-in -law, Andy Stocking, joined the company to run the kitchen

The strength of family involvement in the company is reflected in their long-standing relationships with local craftsman and the strength of their word of mouth reputation. It is a testament to the standard of the company's customer service that some clients are now coming back for their second or third kitchen.

Above: *Just one of the many ranges of quality kitchens the firm can supply.* ***Top:*** *The shop in the early 1990s.*

Bringing colour to Bromley

Whilst serving in the second world war Jack Bollom made plans with one of his comrades to start a company to produce nail varnish after they were demobbed. Unfortunately Jack's comrade was killed but he decided to go ahead with the project anyway, bringing one of his relatives onboard as a partner. They found a disused farm building on Burnt Ash Lane, Bromley and struck a deal to pay a token rent in return for repairing the roof and installing electricity. The pair sunk their £300 savings into a range of vividly coloured dyes and pigments only to find that the essential ingredient Acetone was unavailable. However disaster was avoided by some quick thinking and the purchase of a consignment of linseed oil. This allowed the fledgling company to use its dyes and pigments to produce a range of vividly coloured paints. The nail varnish coloured paints proved to be a great success after the drabness of the war years and were especially popular in the exhibition, display, television and film businesses. They have proved so popular in fact that they still form the basis of the JW Bollom paint range today.

In 1961 the company acquired Henry Flack Ltd. which allowed them to offer a full range of wood finishing products and also enabled them to make the move to their present site at Beckenham. This site has been continually expanded ever since and in 1982 the major production factory was opened by Mr Denis Thatcher.

Along with the brighter paints offered by Bollom's, many of their clients wanted matching fabrics. In 1968 Bollom's began to stock a range of felts in order to meet this need, this was later expanded to include other specialist materials such as suede and hessian. The firm has continued to serve the exhibition and display trade especially from their Old Brompton Road depot in London which is ideally located for supplying the exhibition halls at Olympia and Earls Court.

Bollom's have continued to expand and diversify over the years undertaking ventures into areas such

Above: *The cowshed in Burnt Ash Lane, Bromley where Jack Bollom invested his £300 in 1945.*
Below: *Beckenham head office and works, including the new factory which opened in 1982.*

coatings for Windsor Castle during its rebuilding after the fire in the early 1990s. As recognition for this work their Royal Warrant was extended to cover Fire Protective Coatings. This adds to the Royal Warrants that JW Bollom & Co Ltd already had for the supply of French Polishes and Lacquers, and to the Warrant their subsidiary John T Keep & Sons Ltd has for the supply of paint used on Royal carriages. Jack Bollom himself has also received Royal recognition with an MBE.

Bollom's not only expanded their range of products, but expanded geographically and internationally as well. They now have a chain of depots throughout the UK in order to supply their local clients more quickly; and also have their own distribution network in America, known as Henry Flack International Inc, a company incorporated into Bollom's in 1981. The firm has a number of links with America and in 1999 agreed to produce inks, under licence, for the prestigious American Manufacturer, Rutland.

JW Bollom & Co Ltd, now retailing under the name Bromel, are still a family concern and Jack Bollom, now 84 years old, still goes to work most mornings. However it is his son Martin who conducts most of the day to day operations, whilst his grandson, Danny Rowbotham, is responsible for the groups depots.

Top left: *Denis Thatcher opening the new factory in 1982.* **Left:** *The new factory in the grip of the fire, started by arsonists, which burnt it to the ground in August 1996.* **Below:** *Briwax, one of the firm's most popular ranges.* **Bottom:** *Founder, Jack Bollom, MBE, and son Martin, company chairman, display their royal warrants and U S Accolade.*

as wallpaper and screen printing. One of their most successful areas of expansion has been into paint spraying technology. In 1969 the company purchased Lee Compressors in order to be able to offer a fuller customer backup service with spray hire, repair and sales. Today this has lead to the development of Bollom's spray engineering department which is now the company's second biggest division after paint. This department has undertaken a number of unusual projects including the design, construction and installation of a fully automatic, non-destructive, testing facility to inspect Rolls-Royce aero engines for flaws (cost £165,000). At the other end of the scale Bollom's engineers have also worked with Mars Confectionery to install an airless spraying system to coat a range of confectionery with heated chocolate.

The company also diversified into Fire Protective coatings becoming one of the three leading manufacturers in an area in which Britain leads the world. Bollom's supplied all the flame retardant paints and

Rising to meet the challenge in a disposable world

Paramount Plastics has been around for longer than one might think. It is a family firm based in Beckenham and has been producing plastic injection mouldings for half a century, from the very beginning of the industry. However, it does not rest on its laurels, now creating products which are at the forefront of technological development.

Plastics are especially suitable for the hygiene demanded in the food industry. Having produced the first plastic spoons for the famous Lyons Corner House in the days of London smogs and trams, they now make over thirty million pieces of cutlery per month, many of them destined around the globe for McDonalds Restaurants, the world's largest fast food outlet.

When Paramount was chosen to manufacture scale replicas of the Queen's coronation coach in 1953 each one was hand painted by one particular member of staff. (They have since become collectors' items!) Now the colour and finish department has to deal with thousands of items per week for the drinks trade and to decide whether to foil-block or heat-seal the colour. Eventually most find their way to the supermarket shelves which we peruse as we wander round with our trolley. Then again, the children's drinks containers which look to all the world like shiny metal are the product of injected plastic moulding. Naturally cleanliness, the responsibility of every employee from shop floor worker to top management, is closely checked.

It is therefore, perhaps, no surprise that Paramount Plastics also serves the medical equipment industry. They have to ensure that the one million pieces of equipment produced every month can be relied upon to function reliably, perhaps in a life or death situation. The hermetically sealed pack that the paramedic opens as you lie in the ambulance (God forbid!) may have originated in one of their factories. Boots and the NHS are important customers.

One might come across the firm's products in any number of situations. They virtually pioneered the ferro/plastic fishing weight to reduce lead pollution in our rivers and lakes. And printed drawing pin lids feature in their range, too. And so on.........

Over the last fifty years plastics have replaced metal in many applications. Nowadays the company works closely with designers to create prototypes which possess not only strength but also rigidity, flexibility, lightness or transparency, as circumstances demand. Their technicians then follow the project through all its stages to mass production to make sure that the product fulfills its function appropriately. Paramount has succeeded in winning important military contracts in this field, where great stress is laid on sophisticated, accurate work.

Below: *Station Road, Anerley.*

which each employee undertakes to spend at least ten hours per month in product awareness training. As the most significant assets of the firm are its employees, it pays to show them how critical their actions are in relation to their customers' needs.

Although the factories have been re-located away from Kent, Paramount has retained its head office on the Gardener Industrial Estate in Beckenham. There seems to be little reason that this family firm of two generations standing should not be still producing plastic mouldings or their equivalent in another fifty years' time. No doubt the shape and form of products will change. Packaging and colouring will also be subject to the whims of fashion, but Paramount Plastics seems to be well placed to meet the challenge.

As the business has expanded to cover the whole country and beyond, the company has had to find new sites for its production. It chose Ely, in Cambridgeshire, not far from Cambridge University, where links with the scientific and medical world in the various science parks can be easily made. Naturally these new production sites have to conform to high standards of hygiene and cleanliness from the start of the manufacturing process through to the packaging department. The eighty fully trained staff have to ensure that all goods leave the factories in the very best condition. Then easy access to the motorway network and the ports of Essex and Kent also played an important part in the decision to choose this greenfield site.

In an industry where innovation is constantly demanding new skills and knowledge, Paramount has introduced a staff motivation scheme for every member of the company, in

Top: *The original factory in Anerley Station Road, Anerley.* ***Above left:*** *Packing the finished product in the factory's warehouse.* ***Below:*** *Loading Paramount products for delivery nationwide.*

On course to succeed

Bromley College of Further and Higher Education, with a campus encompassing the main site at Rookery Lane as well as the Old Town Hall in Bromley and the Hawthorn Centre in Penge, represents the future. The college's aim is to provide the widest possible range of education and training opportunities to everyone aged 16 years and over. Yet despite always looking to the future the college can also look to a rich past.

The origins of the College go back to the nineteenth century with the 'Bromley School of Science and Art'. The present college however is built on a site near what was once The Rookery, long the home of the Norman family whose association with Bromley goes back to the 18th century. The first of the family, James Norman, first came to the area in 1755, his son George was a Sheriff of Kent whilst James' grandson became a director of the Bank of England. The last of the family line to live in the Rookery was Archibald Cameron Norman who died in 1948; he was Chairman of the Bromley bench of magistrates and served as an Alderman on Kent County Council.

It was only in 1946 that the house disappeared. The building was occupied by the Air Ministry when a fire broke out in the oldest part of the house which dated from before 1716. Interestingly until around 1840 the house had been known as Bromley Common rather than The Rookery.

*Above: A picture of The Rookery before its sad demise in 1946. **Right:** Students embark on an epic bus trip to Moscow and back in the 60s. **Below:** Staff and students from Bromley Technical Institute pictured in the 50s.*

The present main building was opened in September 1959 and covers what were once long stretches of herbaceous borders and flower beds. It was one of the most delightful sites of any college in England, as on its southern side the windows looked out over the landscaped grounds of the old Rookery estate with its rhododendron surrounded lake in the hollow below and on to the wooded countryside beyond Keston. To the north the area was in the process of being developed by the council for athletics and sports in Norman Park.

A new college was formed by the amalgamation of the two Technical Institutes of Bromley and Beckenham, both small centres before the 1939-45 world war: the Beckenham Institute - being the evening section of the Technical School and sharing its building - and the Institute at Bromley holding its evening classes in the Central School in Wharton Road until a VI flying bomb closed that building in 1944.

Before the war neither Institute had more than 400 evening students on their rolls and the curriculum was very limited, both in the choice of subjects and the standard of work.

Memories of *BROMLEY*

By 1964 the college had over 5,000 students enrolled and the full time teaching staff of just five in 1956 had risen to almost 70, aided by 150 part-time lecturers. The many successful former students include the novelist and film maker, Hanif Kureishi, who was once President of the Student Union.

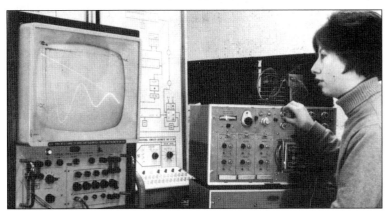

Nowadays, Rookery Lane offers modern laboratories and workshops, a hi-tech language centre, computerised library and a choice of computer suites.

The Old Town Hall in Bromley, occupied in 1995, is where the majority of management training, social work courses and services to business are held whilst the recently refurbished Hawthorn Training Centre on the Groves Estate in Penge provides training in IT, administration and child care amongst other courses.

It was during the war years that more progress was made than had been made in the previous 20 years and by 1944 the joint enrolment had reached over 1,800 students. The range of classes had been extended and the standard of work raised.

The 1944 Education Act envisaged developments in Further Education in both full-time and part time day and evening courses. By 1950 the Institutes had premises of their own. As a matter of convenience the two Institutes developed on distinct lines: engineering and science at Beckenham and commerce and general education at Bromley.

Development was rapid at both Institutes and by 1956 the problem was not how to fill the new college building but how to find even more accommodation with almost 3,000 students enrolled. Fortunately the old Bromley Technical Institute building at Springhill was available for 1960-61 where 250 students could be transferred.

Today the College offers an astonishing range of courses from A levels and NVQs to professional qualifications in subjects as diverse as accountancy and tourism.

Top: *The New Building c1958.*
Above: *Electronics arrive at the College.*
Below left: *An aerial view of the college and its extensive grounds.* ***Below:*** *The Old Town Hall, now home to Bromley College's management training, social work and business studies faculties.*

A long tradition of high quality construction work

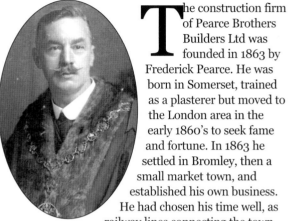

The construction firm of Pearce Brothers Builders Ltd was founded in 1863 by Frederick Pearce. He was born in Somerset, trained as a plasterer but moved to the London area in the early 1860's to seek fame and fortune. In 1863 he settled in Bromley, then a small market town, and established his own business. He had chosen his time well, as railway lines connecting the town with the capital had just been completed, creating a demand for housing and services amongst the new commuters. Lying in the Kent countryside, Bromley proved to be a popular site for the new settlers.

Frederick contributed much to the development of the town, building in the main central streets, and in developing Aldermary Park (now usually known as Sundridge Park).

In the meantime three of his sons had joined the business, which, having established its reputation towards the end of the 19th century, assumed the name of 'Pearce and Sons' and made its headquarters in Sherman Road. As well as speculative building, alteration, repair and maintenance work was now undertaken. Frederick ensured that his sons received a proper training. They were apprenticed at 1/2d. per hour and had to attend evening classes at building school.

present name 'Pearce Bros'. In the first world war Bertram became a Sergeant Major in the Royal Engineers, whilst Sidney remained working in the firm, undertaking work for the Air Ministry towards the end of the war.

In the inter-war period activity expanded. Alongside contract work for local authorities and commercial and industrial concerns, Sidney continued his business with the Air Ministry at aerodromes around London, many of which became household names in the war to come, such as Biggin Hill, Tangmere and Kenley. At Croydon aerodrome, then the main airport for London, Pearce Bros worked on ground installations as traffic increased. Later, they helped prepare the plotting tables for the War Operations Room. During this period a tradition of annual company 'beanos', or outings, was established.

Now enter in 1925 the third generation - Kenneth Pearce - son of Bertram, who began as an apprentice carpenter. As work increased, Pearce Bros moved to new offices in Widmore Road, with works in

When Frederick died in 1903 two of his sons, Bertram and Sidney, continued the business and endowed it with its

Top left: *Bertram Pearce in his mayoral robes.*
Above right: *The hand decorated manuscript awarded to Bertram Pearce at the end of his term of office.*
Right: *Apprentices in 1934.*

raise the efficiency of the whole Construction Industry. Since then Kenneth and his son have been very active in the training and organisation of the industry. Pearce Bros. contributed to the gradual process of regeneration, constructing new housing, schools, factories as the country got back on its feet.

Now enter the fourth generation - Roger Pearce - son of Kenneth, who began his studies, like his forebears, at Brixton School of Building. Having joined the company in 1955, he became director in 1962, being responsible mainly for larger contract work. As the firm went on from strength to strength he rose to Managing Director in 1976 and Chairman 1987 and later his wife became thoroughly involved with the day to day workings.

The fifth generation Andrew Pearce joined in 1986, trained at South East London Technical College, and is now the Director responsible for the Estimating and Supervision. He now looks forward to continuing the tradition of the family in high quality construction work and to the year 2013 when the company will surely celebrate its 150th birthday of service to the community of Bromley.

North Street. As the second world war approached the firm once again took on more contracts for the Air Ministry, as well as constructing air - raid shelters.

The company, still managed by Bertram and Sidney, found the war years difficult. Kenneth was called up and the firm's activities shrank. However, this provided another member of the family with the opportunity to make her mark. Evelyn Pearce, Kenneth's wife, began helping in a part-time capacity, but with her skills she played a major part in the management of the business, which in 1944 became a private limited company. Bertram died in 1945 and Sidney retired from active work, although he continued as a director until his death in 1955.

'Mrs. Ken', as Evelyn was known, now helped to lead Pearce Bros through the post-war period, re-establishing a skilled workforce and re-equipping with new plant and machinery after the firm had gradually run down during hostilities. In 1955 she was appointed director. During this time the company decided to participate in efforts made by the Building Employers to

Top left: The offices at 46 Widmore Road. ***Above left:*** *One of the firm's lorrys in the late 1930s.* ***Below:*** *The offices at 1-1A North Street in 1963, the firm's centenery year.*

Luxurious accommodation with a well connected history

Bromley Court Hotel is situated on the A21 and offers excellent facilities: accommodation, restaurant, conference and banqueting suites, all set in two acres of carefully tended gardens and with easy access to all major transport routes. Heathrow and Gatwick airports are twenty five and thirty miles away respectively. Bromley has two railway stations: Bromley South to Victoria and Bromley North to Charing Cross. The notorious motorway cum 'car park', the M25, is in close proximity to the hotel.

The hotel occupies a site on Bromley Hill that was first built upon around the year 1776. This small villa was purchased in 1801 by well connected MP, Charles Long. He was a lifelong friend of William Pitt the Younger. They worked well together, despite having different views on the slavery problem. It was said that Long was jealous of the influence that the slavery reformer William Wilberforce had over the Prime Minister. In fact, it was Pitt who encouraged Charles Long to purchase Bromley Hill.

This page: *Views to the front and rear elevation of Bromley Hill Place circa 1900.*

Charles Long became a Member of Parliament in 1789 (the time of Mme Guillotine and The Scarlet Pimpernel) and Pitt made him Secretary of the Treasury from 1791 to 1801 and then Secretary of State for Ireland in 1805. Post Master General was Long's next Government position; this job he held from 1807 to 1826.

Pitt's niece, Lady Hester Stanhope remarked, 'Mr Charles Long used to slide in and out; and slide here and slide there; nobody knew where he went or when he came; so quiet.' (Shades of The Pimpernel!)

After the death of Pitt, Long become an adviser to the Prince Regent (later King George IV) who regarded Charles as a useful ally. Charles gaining a reputation as an official qualified to arbitrate on matters of taste and public money. Long married Amelia, the daughter of Sir Abraham Hume, the art fancier and he and Hume became leading figures in cultural circles in London. Amelia was an able amateur artist, producing fine sketches of the Bromley area. In 1816, she made etchings of Bromley Hill for a gift book for friends. It's almost certain that Charles and Amelia Long demolished whatever building was present when they bought Bromley Hill Place and had a villa erected, reflecting their personal desires. Their house was smaller than the present building which incorporates Long's villa, which was Italianate in character with a square tower and circular windows.

The garden, which was exceedingly famous during the time of the Longs, has been totally broken up. Only two large urns have survived and can be seen in the front and rear gardens. A stone terrace has recently been laid at the rear of the hotel. The real glory of Bromley Hill, the view, which once included St Paul's, is present to this day. The ground still slopes sharply, at this point in time, to a thicket of rhododendrons and silver birch, permitting a view over the brow of the hill to the distant delights of our capital city.

The Bromley Court Hotel has been owned by the same family since 1931, and developed into a large modern hotel and conference centre over the years.

The hotel currently consists of 115 bedrooms, all of these have en-suite facilities with satellite television, telephone with modem point and voice mail facilities; tea and coffee, hair driers and 24 hour room service and currently fifteen of the bedrooms are air-conditioned.

Conference facilities consist of nine air-conditioned rooms suitable for interviewing as well as a theatre style presentation suite for up to 150 delegates.

The hotel is licensed for civil marriage ceremonies and has extensive banqueting suites catering for 30 persons up to 190. With the landscaped gardens it offers the perfect setting.

The Garden Restaurant and Conservatory overlooking the rear garden is ideal for private lunches or dinners and is renowned for its weekend dinner dances and traditional Sunday lunches for all the family.

For residents the leisure facilities provide a well equipped gymnasium, spa pool and steam room and is the perfect place to unwind after a long day.

As you would expect from a hotel that is a member of the Best Western Group, you will have a profoundly satisfying experience when you sample the exquisite delights of the Bromley Court Hotel & Conference Centre. Visit the website at www.bromley-hotel.co.uk.

Top: *An interior view of the old conservatory.*
Below: *Bromley Court Hotel today.*

On target for quality

MS Instruments Plc has been at the leading edge of weapon and ammunition testing since 1972. The company's main activities revolve around the design and manufacture of military training equipment and weapons testing systems. It is one of the major suppliers in the world of these highly specialised instruments. The company supplies to armies, navies and air forces as well as to police forces around the world. In 1980 the company's projectile Velocity Measuring System and their Acoustic Target type 530 were selected for use in NATO weapons trials.

Most of the company's off the shelf systems have been designed and built under private finance and the company maintains its equipment with logistics support and an after sales service. The company prides itself on the reliability of its equipment and its low running costs and are dedicated to extended support of their products for a minimum of ten years.

MS Instruments carries out special work to order such as the specialised instrumentation for the light gas gun at DRA Fort Halstead, and equipment for AWRE Foulness. MS Instruments also designed a complete weapons testing facility for Royal Ordnance in Nottingham which has now been in use for over nine years, and the firm also supplied the quality control software for the project. Similar equipment has since been manufactured for other Royal Ordnance sites as

well as for private companies and a number of overseas governments including, Austria, Sweden, India, Malaysia and Egypt. The company's experienced staff pride themselves on their ability to manufacture equipment to suit individual clients and solve complex problems.

Training systems have also been supplied to a number of countries around the world. These systems include the pop-up targets which are so familiar from film and television. Other systems include devices such as the Automatic Marking System (AMS) which enables trainee rifle shooters or gunners to hone their skills. The AMS gives the trainee instant feedback on exactly where their shots hit the target, enabling them to better

Top: *MS Instruments headquarters.*
Right: *Precision flash detector.* **Far right:** *The army using MS Instruments equipment on their training grounds.*

of the Vehicle Hostile Fire Indicator which operates in a similar manner and has initially been developed for use in armoured personnel carriers, with a possible further application on VIP cars.

Many of MS Instruments systems rely upon computers. As part of their manufacturing process the company designs and codes all of the high-integrity scientific software needed to run their equipment.

understand how they performed. These units are designed to be both versatile and rugged enabling them to be used in a wide variety of environments. Similar equipment is also available for aircraft to practice bombing missions. This kind of training equipment has been supplied to the British army, airforce and police. It has also been exported to countries including Qatar, Malaysia, Indonesia, Saudi Arabia, Germany and the Netherlands.

MS Instruments also designs and supplies Night vision systems, over 800 of which have been supplied to the RAF. This system was used by RAF Tornado pilots during the Gulf War, allowing highly successful and accurate low-level attacks to be carried out.

An expanding area of the company's work has been the Hostile Fire Indicator. Originally used by Army Air Corps helicopters in Northern Ireland, this system detects hostile fire and provides the pilot with an alarm and some indication of where the fire is coming from. The system has now been adopted by a number of overseas airforces for use during United Nations peace keeping operations. Over 30 such units are in use with the Italian airforce in the Lebanon. The successes of the Hostile Fire Indicator has lead to the development

Another aspect of the company's activities is the design and manufacture of Image Measurement Systems for industrial quality control. This system uses unique hardware and software to measure complex industrial components quickly and to an extreme accuracy of better than five microns.

The quality of the companies products was rewarded in 1986 by the British Ministry of Defence with the awarding of the NATO AQAP1 Quality assurance standard for both their hardware and software. In 1993 the company was approved to ISO9001 and 9000-3.

As one would expect from a company so dedicated to technology MS Instruments has its own website at www.msinstruments.co.uk. Its website was created in 1995 and was the first of its kind in the industry.

This page: *Moving target practice for HM Forces using targets designed and engineered by MS Instruments.*

A *dedicated service to the people and businesses of Bromley*

The Accountancy Firm of F W Berringer & Co was founded in the early 1930s by Ferdinand William Berringer, a Chartered Accountant, from his home in Pembroke Road, Bromley. Offices were taken up at 8 Widmore Road, Market Square, Bromley in the late 1930s, where the practice continued to grow. From that quiet start, the firm has been part of the business community in Bromley for nearly 70 years and still retains its independent status. Mr Berringer lived and worked in Bromley throughout his life bringing up his four children in the area and also served for a period on Bromley Council in the mid 1950s. After retiring from full time activity in the firm in 1972, he continued as a consultant for some years. He died in 1984.

John Berringer, the son of the founder, joined the firm in 1955, qualified as a Chartered Accountant in 1961 and became a partner in the firm shortly thereafter. He became senior partner on his father's retirement in 1972 and continued in that role until his untimely death in 1998. He was a City Liveryman in The Worshipful Company of Chartered Accountants in England and Wales from the 1970s. In addition to running a busy practice, John Berringer served the local community as a magistrate and played a constructive role in local organisations, including activities as a founder member and treasurer of the Bromley Business Partnership, and treasurer of the Bromley Y Project, a youth counselling service within the borough. Bromley Rotary Club benefited from John Berringer's membership and he was treasurer during the 1980s.

Above: *Company founder Ferdinand William Berringer.*

Below: *Staff pictured in 1983, assembled in the Library at the Institute of Chartered Accountants Hall in Moorgate, London.*

At the same time as John Berringer became a partner, so also did Denis Joyce, following his qualification as a chartered accountant with the firm. Continuing the involvement of partners of the firm within the local community, Denis Joyce became one of the founder members of the Bromley Enterprise Agency Trust which still thrives through to the present time.

The team of John Berringer and Denis Joyce presided over a substantial expansion of the firm during the early 1970s and the pattern of such expansion has continued to the present day.

A new partner, David Harvey, was introduced in 1975 and the three partner team operated until the firm's move to new premises in the early part of 1985.

Part of the business community in Bromley for nearly 70 years

Despite having taken over the adjoining offices in Widmore Road at number 6, the firm's need for new premises grew leading in 1985 the move to the present premises at Lygon House, 50 London Road, Bromley. In these more modern surroundings, the firm continues to expand with John Cardnell, the present senior partner of the firm, becoming a partner in 1986.

Following David Harvey's eventual retirement in 1988, the firm benefited from the admission of Colin Raven as a partner.

In 1991, Denis Joyce retired and was succeeded as a partner by John Corney, who as a fellow of the Association of Authorised Public Accountants, had been manager of the firm for many years since first joining the practice in 1967. In 1999 Gordon Hillier was admitted as a partner, after a long working association with the firm as a sole practitioner.

Following F W Berringer and John Berringer before them the continuing partners each devote substantial time to local affairs, whether it be within Rotary, business organisations or charities within the borough. The current senior partner continues the firm's involvement with The Worshipful Company of Chartered Accountants in England and Wales, as a Liveryman.

In meeting its requirements to serve the business community within Bromley, London and the South East in particular, the firm has developed an effective and experienced tax department under the management of Yvonne Mantle, who joined the practice in 1980, and with the introduction of further partners, Peter Tymms and Roy Mackenzie, F W Berringer & Co is now a six-partner firm.

The pattern of events since the early beginnings has been that incoming partners and staff of the firm have brought in diverse experience from time with city firms, and this experience has blended well with the firm's ongoing philosophy of personal service to its clients in a friendly and constructive atmosphere.

Below: *Today's partners.*

Building bridges across two millennia

With an annual turnover of over $1billion, more than 12 thousand staff and offices throughout the world the locally-based civil engineering firm of Maunsell is little short of a legend.

The firm which bears his name was founded in 1955 when Guy Anson Maunsell was already 71 years old. Guy Maunsell was born in Kashmir. He studied civil engineering in London and in 1909 joined the staff of Easton Gibb & Co helping to build the new naval base at Rosyth.

During the first world war Guy Maunsell served in the Royal Engineers and became involved in the construction of concrete ships. Due to his experience in dock construction, in 1931, he was appointed as construction manager to widen London's Putney Bridge and later became managing director of the Anglo-Danish

construction company building the Storstrom Bridge linking the Danish islands of Lolland and Falster.

During the second world war it was Maunsell who inspired the construction of the famous Mulberry Harbours which were towed across to Normandy after the D-Day landings.

Guy Maunsell died in 1961 his last project being the Gladesville Bridge in Sydney, the largest concrete arch in the world at the time of its construction.

At its birth the new firm had just six staff and only one job - a bridge in Perth Australia; fortunately other work soon followed such as the Tasman Bridge in Hobart, a dry dock in Swansea and a land reclamation scheme in Mozambique. In 1958 another Maunsell design was London's then revolutionary Hammersmith flyover.

In the following decades Guy Maunsell's firm has been involved in hundreds of major building projects from the massive Premier Dry Dock in Singapore to the Hong Kong's Mass Transit Railway.

Projects better known to local people will be the pedestrianisation of Bromley town centre, the highway bridge over Bromley South station which is enclosed with Maunsell's world-leading advanced composite construction system, Docklands Light Railway, Croydon Tramlink and Waterloo to Westminster section of the Jubilee Line.

With its corporate service headquarters in Croydon Road, Beckenham today's firm unquestionably stands as a fitting tribute to the remarkable man who founded it.

Above left: *Guy Maunsell.* ***Left:*** *World War II bombardment towers designed and engineered by Guy Maunsell in 1943.* ***Above:*** *Aberfeldy footbridge, Scotland, the World's first advanced composite footbridge.*

The switchboard operators are hard at it at RAVENSbourne Telephone Exchange, Church Road, in a busy scene from May 1967 *(above)*. In the present age of the mobile phone, when at any one moment large sections of the population seem to have this piece of modern technology glued to their ears, it is easy to forget a time when the possession of a telephone of any sort was much less widespread. And although most people's telephones not so long ago used to look like the one shown at bottom left of the photograph, with which you dialled a number rather than pushed buttons, how quickly they have become almost museum pieces. It was during the rising prosperity of the 1960s that many more people had their first telephones installed, and although the technology at Church Road was as up-to-date as it could be in 1967, the 25 telephonists were still working a manual exchange. There were some 9,000 RAVENSbourne

and 4,000 WIDmore subscibers at this date, and the telephonists dealt with upwards of 3,000 calls per day. The featured switchboard girls were certainly under pressure, working for three or four hours at a time without a break, and with a target of cutting the normal answering time from nine seconds to just over seven seconds. It was maybe a sign of the times that the night shift was worked by an all-male staff, but perhaps not particularly a sign of the times that hoax emergency calls always went up during the school holidays! The mysteries

of how everything actually works in the telecommunications business has always rested in the hands of a skilled few, one of whom is pictured here *(below)*. The gentleman on the stepladder was repairing a line selector, and in May 1967 at the RAVENSbourne Exchange, Mr Irwin Brown was in charge of all such engineering personnel, along with the equipment - an awesome responsibility. The pictured room was one that was packed with wiring and electrical fittings - from floor to ceiling - and every effort was made to exclude dust and damp. The meter room at the Exchange was guarded with strict security in 1967, and specially selected telephonists entered it to read subscribers' meters once every three months. It was a telltale sign of the future that the General Post Office was hoping soon to have a computer to deal with meter-reading. Almost 20 years on, in 1986, it was to be a very different story. The telephone network was now run by the privatised British Telecom, which was promising Bromley a digital exchange by 1987, as part of a programme which was seeing a new one opened almost every day. The directory enquiry system had already been computerised, and customer records, along with a customer service system to deal with complaints and enquiries, was going down the same road. The talk was not so much of wiring as of 'optical fibre cable'. And since then, of course, we have entered the world of mobiles, answering machines and touch-button technology.

A street party at Clock House Road, Beckenham, on May 30th 1945, VE Day.

Acknowledgments

Bromley Libraries

J Topham Picture Library

The Kentish Times

AC Johns

R Copeland

TC Mesher

Muriel Mudie

Thanks are also due to
Peter Thomas who penned the editorial text
and Judith Dennis for her copywriting skills